Taking Root

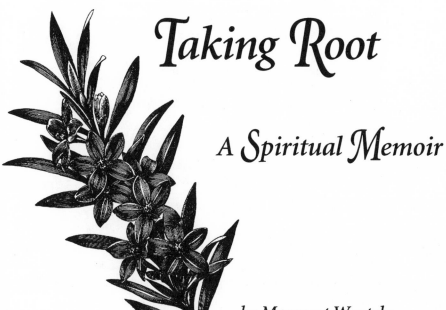

Taking Root

A Spiritual Memoir

by Margaret Wurtele

For Mary –
With much love,
Margaret.
2-12-98

For Angus, whose love and support have
allowed me to grow and thrive.

 Genuine recycled paper with 10% post-consumer waste.
Printed with soy-based ink.

The publishing team included Carl Koch, development editor; Rebecca
Fairbank, copy editor; Amy Schlumpf Manion, production editor; Hollace
Storkel, typesetter; Maurine R. Twait, art director; Gary J. Boisvert, cover
designer; Laura A. Crosby, back cover photo; pre-press, printing, and
binding by the graphics division of Saint Mary's Press.

The inside illustrations are reprinted from *Floral Illustrations: A Treasury
of Nineteenth-Century Cuts,* compiled and arranged by William Rowe
(Mineola, NY: Dover Publications, 1990). Copyright © 1990 by Dover
Publications. Used by permission.

The acknowledgments continue on page 135.

Printed in the United States of America

Printing: 9 8 7 6 5 4 3 2 1

Year: 2006 05 04 03 02 01 00 99 98

ISBN 0-88489-505-X

Contents

Preface   *7*
Prologue   *10*

June
The Pilgrimage to Growth and Egeria's Diary   *21*

July
Saint Augustine and the Nature of Belief   *31*

August
Seeking Balance and the Rule of Saint Benedict   *41*

September
Out of Death, New Life: Julian of Norwich   *51*

October
Letting Go: Meister Eckhart   *59*

November
Forming Roots in Humility with Catherine of Siena   *67*

December
Wintering: John of the Cross   *74*

January
Exploring the Interior Castle with Teresa of Ávila   *82*

February
For the Glory of God: Martin Luther   *91*

March
Of Seeds and Quaker Silence   *101*

April
Blooming: Dorothy Day   *112*

May
Thomas Merton and the Walls of Freedom   *121*

Epilogue   *130*

Preface

On 14 August 1995—after the completion of this manuscript—
I learned that my son, Phil, had been killed in a mountain-climbing
accident. He was twenty-two years old, a summer ranger at Mount
Rainier National Park.

On the night of 12 August, he and another young ranger had
been assigned to a rescue mission. As they inched their way up the
slippery terrain, the weather turned very cold and icy. Just before
midnight, at 13,200 feet—just 300 feet from their destination—
bound together with ropes, they fell to their death. My life—as a
mother, as a woman, as a writer—divides at that point. There is
before, and there is after. Saint John's Dark Night arrived with a
vengeance.

I reached out for hands to hold, and there were many. I turned,
of course, to my friend Nancy, but she learned within a week of
Phil's death that she had ovarian cancer. Eleven months later, on 30
June 1996, she too died, after a long, brave, and creative dance with
her disease.

I questioned the wisdom of publishing this book. So much
had changed, I thought. I seemed to be an entirely new person,
redefined and reoriented by these losses. My life now is about
healing, about learning to live without my only child and my oldest
friend. The book I would write today would be an entirely different
one.

On the other hand, I have been helped to see that this is a
story that needs to be told. The process of coming alive spiritually
was timely and valuable, and it gave me the tools I would not have
had before to cope with shock, grief, and loss. The insights I have
gained through these years of discovery have shaped my thinking
and enlarged my vocabulary, so that I am better able to absorb the
pain and redirect the energy of grief into new directions for the

future. My ability to let go has been put to the ultimate test. In this crucible, I am searching for the forms that resurrection will take.

I found a passage in my journal that has paved the way for recovery. Three years before my son's death—when Phil was nineteen and a sophomore in college—a friend of his, a high school soccer teammate, was killed in a car accident on Christmas Eve. Phil returned home from the memorial service a few days later. His friend had been his mother's only child too, and he looked at me with tears running down his cheeks and said, "Mom, all I could think of during the service was you and what would happen to you if anything ever happened to me."

I recorded this encounter in my journal, never dreaming that his fears would be realized. Reading those words now, however, tells me with clarity and certainty that the last thing Phil would want is for me, for my spirit, to die too. He would want me to carry on, to be the Mom he loved—happy and fulfilled—and to live life to the fullest, for both of us.

Besides, Phil read this book. He loved it, and he would be proud to know it had found its way into the world.

Acknowledgments

This book was first written as a synthesis project in the master's in liberal studies program at Hamline University in Saint Paul, Minnesota. I wish to thank my three advisers, all of whom were critical to the book's evolution and have become my friends. Timothy Polk delighted me with his lively classroom teaching, guided and challenged me with theological rigor, and sustained me with his wonderful sense of humor. Edward Sellner, of the College of Saint Catherine, in his course on Christian spiritual history, inspired the original journal on which this book is based and had the vision and enthusiasm to encourage the publication of this larger work. Larry Sutin urged me to new depths with his probing questions, and with his considerable critical and editorial skills, he improved the book immeasurably.

I am so grateful to Saint Mary's Press for publishing the book, and I thank my editor, Carl Koch, for his thoughtful and sensitive suggestions.

Finally, the book would not have been possible without the support of my family and friends. I am grateful to all those who read the manuscript and shared their responses with me, and to my partners at Hungry Mind Press for their encouragement, especially Gail See for insisting that I find a publisher and for helping to make it happen.

Prologue

Stirrings

A cool breeze stirs, reminding me that it is still only May, that summer has not yet officially arrived. I sit back and wipe the sweat from my forehead, being careful to keep my mud-caked fingers away from my skin. It has been a long, hard Saturday afternoon, but after several trips to the nursery and hours of raking, cultivating, digging, and planting, the garden is finally in. I am tired from the effort of it all, but I am satisfied with the rows of tiny plants, secure in their new beds.

I look at these fragile seedlings on their slender stems—each with only a small cluster of thin roots, two or three leaves, and no buds to speak of—and, though I can imagine the color and lushness that July and August will bring, my heart feels more in tune with these new young plants than with the full-grown flowers they will eventually become. I am like these seedlings, I think to myself. I need time to take root, to grow slowly.

I stand up and wipe my muddy hands on the sides of my jeans. I bend down and straighten one of the new snapdragons that has already slumped to the earth. Such small wisps of root, I think, so vulnerable. There is nothing there yet to grip the earth, to hold up and feed a plant of any consequence.

I reach for the hose to give the garden its first drink of the year, and as the gentle spray sends out rivulets of water that settle into tiny pools at the foot of each plant, it is as if I too am receiving the life-giving moisture, absorbing it eagerly into my thirsty spirit. I need time. I need light and sun and nourishment, and I need rest. I need to take all these changes I have been through and simply let them work on me, let them take root.

These last eight years or so have been momentous ones for me, rich with change, dizzying in intensity. At age forty, I left a full-time career in order to spend more time with my son, Phil, in his last years at home before leaving for college. As a teenager intent on forging his independence, Phil was ambivalent about my increased presence at home. Just knowing that I was more available for him, however, made me more at peace with our coming separation.

By the time he left for his freshman year, I felt good about the years we'd had together, and though I was sad to see him go, I was ready for the empty nest and excited about my newfound independence, for the time I would have to pursue my own agenda and my own burgeoning interests. What I did not know was that those years at home, the flexibility and time I had created for the sake of my son, would radically alter my view of the world.

A Secular Start

Until then I had lived an entirely secular life. In fact, I grew up in a household where religion was a dirty word. As young marrieds, my parents were fiercely independent. They were intellectuals, and religion—especially the unthinking, status-seeking Protestantism of their own parents—was decidedly not for them. My legacy took the form of antireligious bias: religious people are weak people; intelligence and dogma do not mix; members of the clergy are hypocritical; and, because we can never "know" the answers to questions of the spirit, it is enough to focus on service to humanity. I received from those same parents strong ethical guidance, stripped of any notions of original sin, shame, or guilt. Without reference to a higher power, they taught me to love life, to appreciate nature, to commit myself to service, and to value human relationships.

As a child, I was often embarrassed by my family's agnostic stance, by our Sunday mornings that centered on a breakfast of waffles and a thorough reading of the newspaper. I longed to go to church so that I could be like everyone else. To please me, my parents tried the Unitarian Society for several years, but the curriculum at Sunday school focused on nature and the religions of other countries. It was better than nothing, but it still left me feeling deprived.

I have a yellowed newspaper clipping from the front page of the *Minneapolis Star*, 2 March 1955. Under the series headline "What Our Religion Means to Our Family" is a photograph of my parents, my younger sister, and me—age nine, all smiles—gathering firewood in the woods near our house. "Our religion is 'man-centered,' based on faith in the dignity and worth of each individual," my mother is quoted as saying. "We believe that progress toward a better society must come through man's efforts alone, not from something outside of nature or supernatural. . . . We believe that the girls can acquire feelings of piety and awe without relating religion to the supernatural. . . . Unitarianism is not an easy thing," she goes on. "It furnishes no ready-made faith upon which to call for comfort in times of crisis. Rather, it calls upon the individual to seek his own inner resources—in a word, his maturity—in such times of stress."

Unitarianism had no creed, but the corollaries of these words became gospel in our household, and I was no heretic. "God," if there was such a thing, was not in the family lexicon. Such a concept was supernatural and an unacceptable explanation for feelings of awe. Other religions were "easy," offering comfort to those who were weak enough to need it. For the mature person, the self-reliant individual, no such balm was necessary.

I was a first child and not inclined to rebel. My parents are engaging, persuasive people, and I simply adopted these biases as the hallmarks of intelligence. I forgot my early longings and went on to Smith College, well grounded in the agnosticism my friends and I all professed during late-night dormitory sessions. I was clearly drawn, though, to abstract thought. I majored in philosophy, but the pursuit of ultimate questions was always rational, an exercise of the head—closer to science than to spirit.

Taken by Surprise

At age twenty-one, I married my high school boyfriend. He too had been raised as a Unitarian, and one of our earliest bonds was a feeling of superiority to our religious friends. We spent two years in the Peace Corps, a year in New York, and then returned to Minneapolis to settle into what I assumed would be a lifetime of wedded bliss. Three years later, our son was born, and as far as I was concerned, I had everything I had ever wanted.

When I was nearly thirty, my husband of seven years announced that he didn't love me any more. We had married too young, he said. I was too headstrong for him, too controlling, not dependent enough. He had never lived on his own. He needed his freedom, needed to "sow his wild oats," needed to be rid of me.

Our son had just turned one. My husband's announcement came from nowhere and took me by surprise. I had thought our marriage was fine and had expected that—like my parents—we would be together for a lifetime. We had been through our college years and the Peace Corps together. We shared a sense of humor, a house, a dog, a name, and a baby. My husband was my life, and now he was leaving.

Months followed—months of despair—but eventually I began to move on. For the first time in my life, I was on my own. For someone who had moved directly from high school to college to marriage, being on my own was an entirely new experience. I got a job raising money for a united arts fund in Saint Paul. It was only four days a week, so I could devote the other three days to my son. Along with my paycheck came a growing sense of self-reliance and pride. I had worked before Phil was born, of course, but my job had been only for "self-fulfillment." My husband's check was the "real" one, the one that paid the mortgage and put food on the table. Now I was buying groceries, clothes, gasoline, and heat out of money I had earned. It was exhilarating.

I had my son to look after, but he was a joy as well. He went to a day-care center. He had devoted grandparents, an aunt who doted on him, and a father—all who took him willingly and often. I began to find time, time alone that I had never experienced before. Instead of dreading nights by myself, I began to look forward to them.

Staying Busy

Three years after my divorce, when my son was four, I married Angus, a man eleven years my senior who had three children. Even though Angus had been raised as an Episcopalian, a friend of ours, a judge, performed the ceremony, and the *New York Times* became the focus of our Sunday mornings. Angus had not attended church regularly for years, and he readily accepted my secular orientation.

I thought religion would not be an issue in our marriage, but I was soon to find it was not so simple.

Before we were married, Angus had established a New Year's Eve ritual in which he looked back over the year just passed and examined each of the categories of his life. I liked the idea, and one year I suggested that we do it together and read our reflections out loud. As he was reading his to me, he came to a category called spiritual. He said that he felt he was neglecting this aspect of his life and wished he could bring more focus to it in the coming year. I looked at him blankly. "I can't help you there," I said. "I don't even have that category."

We carried on as before, however, and the next decade was a busy, satisfying one. I had a full-time career with the Dayton Hudson Foundation, and Angus was an executive at Valspar, a growing paint and coatings manufacturing company. Each morning I left home, often before breakfast, and went to my desk in an office tower in downtown Minneapolis. I usually had meetings during the lunch hour, and, even though the workday was officially over at five, I nearly always brought home a briefcase full of reports and grant applications that needed to be read in the relative leisure of home. Often I had to attend performances by theaters or music organizations seeking grants, so many of my nights were devoted to work as well.

Four children were living at home in those days. My step-children, two boys and a girl, were busy teenagers with lives full of sports, homework, and social activities. My own son was not yet in high school and needed someone to watch his hockey games, go to his piano recitals, deliver him to friends' houses or dentist appointments, and be available to him in countless ways. I constantly felt guilty that I couldn't give any of the children as much time as they deserved. There was never enough of it. My husband and I had to cook dinner, do the dishes and the grocery shopping, attend to household chores, and maintain the yard, the cars, the dog. There was no end to the demands on us, and with two full-time jobs, something had to go. That "something" was solitude and any time for self-examination or a search for the meaning of it all. I thrived on activity. I was energized, accomplished, and inclined to control; life seemed to be a satisfying series of tasks that I could simply do.

Turning Point

Occasionally, like abnormal blips on a cardiovascular readout, there were signs of change. For example, I loved the arts. I had worked for a museum in my first job, and later raised money for the united arts fund. At Dayton Hudson, our giving program directed much of its support to the arts. Something touched me about the impulse that moved a composer, a painter, or a poet to create a work of art. I knew what it was to receive a work of art directly, to resonate with the artist's impulse, and I came back again and again in search of those moments: in museums or concert halls, in the theater, in books. It would never have occurred to me to name or think of this response as spiritual.

One day when I was traveling with my young son to visit my grandmother in Tucson, our plane was delayed in Denver. I found myself sitting next to a man in the waiting area, and we struck up a conversation. He was lively, intelligent, and sensitive. I can't remember what was said, but when they announced the plane's departure a couple of hours later, I was surprised at how fast the time had gone. "By the way, what do you do?" I asked him as we parted, wondering what could be the life work of this man so full of warmth and wisdom. "I am the Episcopal bishop of Minnesota," he replied. I boarded the plane, amazed that he was a member of the clergy, wondering if we would meet again.

As I neared the end of my thirties, everything began to change. I had begun to be obsessed with my title, with the size of my paycheck, and I realized that though I loved my job, I was not finding the satisfaction in the work that I once had. I knew I needed a new challenge, but I was not sure what I wanted to do next. Angus's children had all gone off to college, and I realized my own son would be gone in five years. It scared me. I felt as if motherhood was going too fast, that if I didn't find some time to spend with him, I would have missed too much of the most important thing in my life.

On 27 November 1984, I wrote the following in my journal:

> I have just finished reading May Sarton's *Journal of a Solitude*, closing the book with tears in my eyes. "We are one," she says, "the house and I, and I am happy to be alone—time to think, time to be. This kind of open-ended time is the only luxury

that really counts. . . . The most valuable thing we can do for the psyche, occasionally, is to let it rest, wander, live in the changing light of a room, not try to be or do anything whatever."

How can I express what this book has given me? Nothing remarkable . . . a simple telling of a simple life . . . but a life so centered, so mellow, so rich that I can only close my eyes and long to find the same tranquility.

The good news is I have choices. I know I can do whatever I decide to do. But deciding is the trick. I must open myself to every possibility, then see where I end up. I believe that my direction will become clear, that it will reveal itself to me, but I must cultivate the medium, the fertile inner environment to let it happen. Oddly, part of letting it happen is doing nothing. I need to disengage a bit—let go, relax, put everything out of focus and see what emerges.

Luckily my paycheck was not critical to our family finances. One night I dreamed of diving off a high dive, and the next day I decided to quit my job, to strip myself of the title I had become obsessed with, and to create an island of time—time to spend with my son and time to spend with myself.

I left Dayton Hudson in June of 1985. I was terrified that I would never find another job and terrified of facing life without a title, wondering what I would say when people asked me, "What do you do?" But I did it. For the first time since my son was a baby, I spent the summer with him, without baby-sitters, day camps, or summer programs. I began to garden in earnest, to read more, and to study yoga.

Because I had more time during the day, I took regular walks. I began to notice, on a daily basis, which new green shoots were emerging from the ground, which plants coming into flower. I walked, rain or shine, and I developed a sensitivity to the weather, to the nuances of the day. I began to need these periods more and more, whether walking or doing yoga, interludes when the rest of my life was put on hold. As I slowed the mental chatter, halted the questions, the worries, the anxieties, the plans, my mind would enter a suspended state and come to a sort of stillness. It was as if a switch was pulled, and when that switch was pulled, I was refreshed. Those episodes lent a certain resonance to everything else, as if "I" stepped out of the driver's seat, and what was left was not a void but another kind of consciousness, a different realm. It had no name, no structure, but I found I needed more and more to ground myself in that other realm, to create a solid base that would carry me over and undergird the active part of my life.

Taking the Next Steps

Five years passed. I resumed an active life, but instead of working full-time, I took on part-time, project-oriented work. I became active with my son's school, with the Guthrie Theater, with a nonprofit press, but I preserved in all these activities the flexibility of time. I managed to keep up the yoga classes, the walks, and the reading.

I read *The Road Less Traveled*, by the psychiatrist M. Scott Peck, an adult convert himself, in which he suggested that it was possible and not uncommon to "mature into a belief in God." Until then I had accepted my parents' admonitions that the mature, self-reliant individual did not need the crutch that religion represented. Peck helped me get over the shame I felt at my growing spiritual inclinations.

I watched a series of interviews on public television with Joseph Campbell, who spoke about the importance of myth in all the cultures of the world. He suggested that by mining the truths of myth as found in religion, and particularly by choosing one tradition and entering deeply into it, one could achieve a deeper level of self-awareness and find valuable opportunity for reflection.

I was drawn to Eastern religious thought from the study of yoga, but I have never been inclined to be a fish out of water. I was wary of choosing a path that was grounded in an entirely different culture. Christianity, however, was a little closer to home. My parents, though they had rejected the tradition, had been brought up as Christians. I had attended a private school during my high school years. It was not a religious institution but had required attendance three times a week at chapel, where we recited the Lord's Prayer and sang Christian hymns. I had lived the rhythm of a Christian year all my life, celebrating secular versions of Christmas and Easter. My husband was, after all, raised as an Episcopalian. Did it not make sense to see if Christianity would work?

Initially I thought it could not. The very word *Christian* suggested a stereotype with which I could not bear to identify. I revived all my early biases and then some. I envisioned a sanctimonious, self-righteous person who saw only the worth of her own religious tradition. I thought I would have to adopt the notion of a personal God, an old man with a white beard who would judge me and mete out the consequences of my actions. I imagined I would have to attest to the "facts" that Jesus was both man and divine, that he physically rose from the dead, that he was sitting somewhere up in heaven, and that I would eventually come face-to-face with him after my own death.

I read Alan Watts's book *Myth and Ritual in Christianity*. In it he tells the Christian story as myth, apart from its relation to historical facts. He takes the reader through the Christian year, describing the rituals as they relate to the story. I began to see that I could accept Christian teachings as metaphor, that I could absorb the Scriptures and liturgy without applying the tests of intellect, and that I could use their wisdom as a touchstone, a source of insight and revelation.

I worked up my courage and wrote a letter to the Episcopal bishop of Minnesota, my friend from the Denver airport. He responded with eagerness and warm support, and began meeting with me on a regular basis. Later that year, at the age of forty-six, I was baptized and then confirmed in the Episcopal church.

The bishop has been the one to fire my imagination. He has taught me to welcome paradox, to be comfortable with contradiction, to listen with my heart, and to receive the messages of myth and metaphor. He has recommended books with uncanny sensitivity and timing; he has encouraged me to keep writing. Most of all, he has listened profoundly, with attention and without judgment. He has been the window through which light has broken.

The bishop was not my only support. Nancy, for example, has been my close friend for thirty-five years. As a teenager, I watched her active life in the Congregational church with fascination: youth retreats, a theater group, her admiration for her ministers. When she was in her late thirties, Nancy went to seminary to pursue a degree in counseling that has led to a career in spiritual direction. I was irritated by the changes this brought about in her language and by the growing intensity of her commitment to the spiritual life.

Though our friendship remained strong, I knew there was a potential gulf of understanding that could threaten our relationship.

I don't believe Nancy ever tried to convince me to change or even made an effort to induce me to see things her way. I only know that as I began to open up, to "thaw out," as she once put it, she was a constant source of positive reinforcement. She reassured me that my tears were not pathological but therapeutic. She recommended books. She gently suggested words that helped me to express what I was feeling. She offered example after example from her own life that mirrored my strange new experience, and she always promised that the rewards of the direction I was headed were worth the price I was paying in uncertainty and chaos.

Listening to Another Voice

It has all happened so fast and is still so new. This is an era of instant gratification, so part of me thinks this period of confusion and growth should all be over. You've read enough now, this voice says. You've been going to church for over two years; you've been doing yoga for nearly seven. It's time to stop navel gazing and get on with your life.

And yet there is another voice, a stronger one, that knows the changes have only just begun. This voice stops me from saying yes to projects that threaten to keep me busy but not fulfilled. I find this voice turning down invitations to parties where the people will be unable to understand what I am about these days. I'm still the same cheerful me most of the time, but my feelings are close to the surface. When I talk to people—either old friends or new acquaintances—I often feel as if the air between us has mysteriously thinned. I see things in their eyes and sometimes understand what they are thinking before they say it. I need time for reflection. A day of busyness leaves me feeling depleted, uncentered.

This process of spiritual growth, of conversion, has a life of its own, I find. Changes come, work goes on within me, and I am often surprised, wondering at these unfolding gifts of grace. On the other hand, I have fed the process and deliberately let myself be nurtured by mentors, both living and dead, by friends, by members of the clergy, and by figures I have encountered in books.

I enrolled in a master's in liberal studies program at a local university shortly after my son left for college. Designed for working adults, the classes were held on weeknights and Saturdays. I signed up with the intention of studying literature, but before I knew it, I was instead taking classes in creative writing and religion. I took a course on the history of Christian spirituality, one that explored the classic texts of the Christian tradition from the early mothers and fathers of the desert all the way to Thomas Merton in the twentieth century.

From this treasure house of wisdom, this great cloud of witnesses, I have identified certain favorites whose writing I wish to explore in greater depth. Month by month in the next year, I will reflect on those whose writing has touched me in some way and with whom I feel a connection in my own spiritual development. As the year goes on, I will reflect as well on the passing of the seasons, both in the garden and in the liturgical calendar, and see how they relate to what I have been reading and to me. As I contemplate the words of these men and women, I will hold them up to the mirror of my own life and work. I want to go back and discover the roots of this new way of life that I have chosen. Like the seedlings in my new summer garden, I need to let their wisdom seep into my spirit like rain into deep, porous soil.

The Pilgrimage to Growth and Egeria's Diary

The only thing I can count on in the garden is change. Nothing is the same from one day to the next. Having chosen and planted each of the seedlings myself, I get to know them well, and I can literally monitor their growth every twenty-four hours. A new leaf on the blue salvia, a bud on the white petunia. At this time of year, each day is full of surprises and visible progress. Later, at the end of the summer, the change will be of a different kind: a withered blossom, a blackened stem, the beginnings of decay. Each plant has its own life and follows a unique itinerary.

So it is with me. It's far less obvious from day to day, but I too change and grow, unfolding inexorably, playing out a life that sometimes seems to go according to plan, at other times to be nothing more than a game of chance. I have always been interested in charting my own progress. Fascinated by the twists and turns of my life, I have kept journals since I was in junior high school—not records of daily events, but books of occasional entries that reflect on significant turning points: a new relationship of interest, a trip of any consequence, the beginnings of dissatisfaction with a job, the frustrations of marriage or motherhood. These last few years of upheaval, of radical change and spiritual awakening, have been chronicled in more frequent entries, examined in greater depth than ever before. All my life I have heard of the "spiritual journey," and, though I would prefer to avoid the hackneyed term, it seems particularly applicable to the open-ended, adventurous nature of this pilgrimage of mine to I-know-not-where.

This urge of a woman to record her life, to preserve the path she has traveled, is not new. There is in fact a journal that survives from the late fourth or early fifth century describing a woman's expedition to Egypt, Jerusalem, and other parts of the Holy Land. *Egeria: Diary of a Pilgrimage* is a chronicle of the writer's three-year pilgrimage to see and experience firsthand many of the sites referred to in the Scriptures and liturgy.

Who was this Egeria, sometimes known as Aetheria or Echeria, depending on the manuscript, and when did she make such a determined and courageous journey? Scholars are not sure. Current research dates her pilgrimage to sometime between 394 and 417 C.E. She may have been a nun or even an abbess, for much of her journal is in the form of a letter and refers to her "sisters" at home. Her status as a member of a religious community is by no means certain, but it is clear that she sought out and was welcomed by monks wherever she traveled.

Historians speculate that whether or not she was a nun, she was someone of relatively high rank who could use contacts to obtain the military escorts and official assistance that were necessary to make her perilous way through the desert. We don't even know her country of origin. She wrote in Latin, but examination of the language has revealed only the most tenuous hints as to her roots: perhaps the French province of Aquitaine, or Galicia in northwestern Spain.

We can only speculate as well on what motivated Egeria's journey. As a reader, I searched in vain to find hints as to what had prompted her, but the document contains only a straightforward, factual account of the places she visited, the people she met, and the sights she saw. The first section of her diary has been lost. Perhaps in those pages she would have filled us in. Was she tired of community life and seeking solitude in the desert? Was she a liturgical scholar looking for historical background? Was she in a phase of self-examination in her middle years, curious about the roots of her own spirituality?

The portions of Egeria's diary that survive are in two sections. The opening twenty-three chapters begin in the midst of her travels in the Near East and describe several specific expeditions and then her return trip to Constantinople. The last twenty-six chapters describe the customs and liturgy of the church of Jerusalem, especially the rituals and festive celebrations surrounding Lent, Holy Week, and Easter. This eyewitness account of life in the Holy Land at the turn of the fifth century has been a valuable resource for geographers, archaeologists, and scholars of church history. It has helped locate specific biblical sites and provided evidence of some of the earliest forms of Christian liturgy.

We do not know the size of Egeria's entourage, nor can we be sure of its exact itinerary. The land through which she chose to travel was barren, and the terrain rugged and challenging. "At times," she wrote, "the route is through the desert. . . . There is no road there at all, only the sands of the desert all around." The group had to climb mountains on foot. Water was scarce. Egeria focused mainly on the biblical sites she was searching for, so she recorded little else in the way of detail about her trip: the distance between places, the time it took to get there, or precise observations about the landscape or sights along the way.

Her travels took her on a pilgrimage to Mount Sinai, and she retraced the route of the Exodus. She visited Mount Nebo, the mountain that Moses ascended to view the land of Canaan just before he died (Deuteronomy, chapters 48–52). She went to see the tomb of Job at Carneas in Hauran. She took a detour to the tomb of Saint Thomas the Apostle in Edessa, and she visited the house of Abraham in Carrhae and next to it the well from which Rebekah drew water for the camels of his servant (Genesis 24:15).

What seemed to drive Egeria in her travels was a desire to confirm her faith and bring it to life through personal contact with the physical sites of the stories in the Bible. She also wanted to meet a group of people about whom she had heard and whom she greatly respected: the monks who lived in Sinai, Palestine, Mesopotamia, and Isauria. These men and women lived in solitary desert cells and tended the various holy places and churches scattered throughout the region.

On her visit to Abraham's house, for example, Egeria was blessed: "It was our very good fortune and quite beyond our expectations that we saw there the truly holy men of God, the Mesopotamian monks, those men whose reputation and way of life is spoken of far from here." These monks come down out of the hills only one day a year other than Easter, and it was on that very day, the feast of the martyr Saint Helbidius, that Egeria's entourage arrived. The men "consented very readily to receive me," and directly after nightfall returned to their solitary cells.

On another pilgrimage, Egeria went via Tarsus into the region of Isauria in search of the shrine of Saint Thecla, a woman who, according to the apocryphal Acts of Paul, was converted by Paul on his mission to Iconium. At the holy church, Egeria writes, there were "countless monastic cells for men and women." She spent two days there, visiting and praying with those dedicated sisters, before returning to Tarsus.

Egeria and the members of her entourage marked their arrival at every site they visited with the performance of a ritual: "Whenever we were empowered to reach our destination, it was always our custom first to say a prayer, then to read a passage from the Bible, sing a Psalm fitting the occasion, and finally say a second prayer." This practice served to acknowledge her progress, to orient the site at hand in relation to biblical history and tradition, and—most important—to allow her to pause and reflect consciously to give the moment weight and significance.

Sadly, the content of these considerations must be left to the reader's imagination. Such a pilgrimage must have had a profound effect on this courageous woman, and the reader is left longing for some personal reflection that would reveal its ultimate value for her.

I set out in response to a spiritual awakening, and I am propelled by questions that drive me both forward and backward in time. Like Egeria, I am searching for the roots of my tradition in Christian spiritual history, but for me, the points of interest on the way are not geographic but literary: the written works of mystics and religious thinkers over the centuries who have grappled with the same questions that are obsessing me. Presumably Egeria's journey was circular. When she had completed her tour, she returned home to absorb what she had seen. In my case, there is only movement forward and growth from every encounter along this road that leads I know not where.

Most of the seedlings in my garden are annuals, plants that die at the end of a Minnesota growing season and must be restarted by seed or tiny plants in the spring of each year. Another kind of plant, however, anchors the garden. These are perennials, which survive our cold winters, dying back in the fall and living underground to come up again when the weather turns warm in the spring. I stare eagerly at the soil each year in the places I know they are buried, waiting for signs of their re-emergence into the light. I am impressed with the tenacity and strength of their fleshy shoots, for they must negotiate their way from the dormant roots, up through several inches of just-thawed soil. Occasionally they must dislodge small rocks and, finally, manage a mighty thrust to break open the hardened crust of topsoil to emerge in the first stages of growth into a flowering plant.

Often it is just such a groundbreaking that is necessary to launch a journey of the kind Egeria undertook to the Holy Land or that I have begun in my spiritual quest. Even with strong motivation to explore her roots, Egeria must have broken through tremendous obstacles to set off on such a pilgrimage. Were her sisters sympathetic, or did they think she was insane to risk her life in the desert on such a trip? Did she have to work for months to convince her superiors to let her go? How did she obtain the money for the expedition? Could she arrange in advance for the supplies she needed? How did she muster the will to break out of her daily routine, to overcome her fears of the unknown?

This notion of a physical groundbreaking suggests the kind of upheaval that conversion can cause in our life. Far from business as usual, responding to a call to spiritual growth can feel like an earthquake. It can mean allowing the groomed surface of our life to be cracked from beneath, turned over, and shoved aside to make way for growth that is powerful, inexorable, and transforming. In my own case, coping with the spiritual awakening I have undergone in the last couple of years has necessitated a less dramatic departure than Egeria's, but it has involved some difficult dynamics nonetheless.

My relationship with my parents, for example, has changed. I suspect it has been hard for them, having lived so long with their antireligious biases, to have their daughter suddenly embark upon such a spiritual path. My mother has made a particular effort to understand. She has listened carefully to me, and she has even begun asking herself whether there is something in her own study of karate and tai chi that indicates a spiritual bent. If she is receptive to the spiritual nature of my recent changes, though, she still has a difficult time with my decision to become a Christian. She hearkens back to her stereotype of Christians as psychologically needy people who are seeking comfort instead of challenge, and who have a negative and unhealthy preoccupation with their own sinfulness. She is reminded of fundamentalists who loudly proclaim their brand of Christianity even as they perform decidedly unchristian acts of intolerance and even violence. She stops short of ridicule. She loves and respects me too much for that, but I would guess that she is simply tolerating this stage I am going through and waiting until I come around to a healthier, more neutral and universalist position.

If my father acknowledges and nurtures a spiritual dimension in his life, he has never let me know it. He finds it easier simply to ignore what is going on with me. We had lunch together shortly after my confirmation. He listened patiently to my story, but he has never raised the subject again. At another lunch several months later, I mentioned that I had spent the weekend at a retreat entitled Christian Zen. He acted as if he had not heard what I said and then launched into a cheerful line of conversation on another topic altogether.

My parents and I have been unusually close. They are young, and because my husband is right in between my age and theirs, we have many friends in common. I have not had to leave them in any literal sense. I have, though, experienced real sadness that this turning of mine has created a whole arena in which we cannot really communicate and do not share a basic level of understanding. I did not invite them to my baptism or my confirmation, and I have not regretted that decision. I love them, and we have much in common. Still, I have broken new ground, and there is no turning back.

My husband, unlike my parents, began by welcoming these changes in me. After that New Year's Eve encounter shortly after we were married, he accepted my secular orientation, and he only occasionally followed his own bent by going to church alone. When I took confirmation classes last year at the Episcopal cathedral, he came along with me, anxious to reconnect with his old tradition, eager to see what changes, if any, the intervening years had wrought. Soon, though, he began to worry.

My enthusiasm was exceeding conventional bounds. I was reading far too much, taking too many classes, and thinking too much about it all. Though he gladly went with me to church on Sundays, he was nervous that I couldn't let it go at that. When I talked to him about the growing communications gap with my parents, he was afraid he was next. I began to do more of my reading and writing when he was not at home, to hold back occasionally and avoid thinking out loud about the questions that haunted me.

Time has been a healer. He knows now that I am not going to leave him or become a different person. He has told me that he is glad to be going to church again and that he has learned from our conversations about questions of the Spirit. He said he is more comfortable now that he can freely acknowledge his own spiritual side. Still, I have learned in this process that each person's journey is ultimately a solitary one. Even if Angus were to embark on a spiritual quest of equal intensity, it could never be entirely in sync with mine.

❧

Egeria's fifth-century pilgrimage, like any other, encountered both barriers and boosts along the way. On the one hand, Egeria and her companions had to face the physical difficulty of the trip, but on the other, they were greeted at every turn with the generous hospitality of monks, bishops, and other holy people who welcomed them and showed them the historic sites.

The barriers that we encounter on the spiritual path may, like the desert, be external: the resistance of family and friends who may be wary of, or threatened by, change; busy lives that deprive us of time for solitude or spiritual disciplines; or an institutional church that seems more focused on its own politics than on supporting individual spiritual growth. But the barriers may just as well be internal too: skepticism and the need to apply tests of rationality and practicality; a desire to conform, to blend in and not rock the boat; laziness; a competitive and willful nature that keeps us from surrender; or a fear of the unknown.

I have experienced all these barriers, but I have also been aided and abetted by my own version of the monks of the desert. Many of my friends have become fellow travelers with whom I talk regularly, share books, and trade insights. I have benefited from the guidance of my clergy, classroom teachers, and my friend the bishop, with whom I have met regularly. A pilgrim—like Egeria or like me—is an obvious presence on the road, and help is there to be acknowledged and received.

Just as Egeria stopped at every site she visited to perform a series of rituals that marked her progress, I too have found in my own quest that ritual is of critical importance. My baptism and confirmation in the Episcopal church allowed me to stop along the way, to acknowledge that I had reached a point of decision and choice, and then, through time-honored liturgy, to give the moment weight. Through the experience of these sacraments, I could see that though I was clearly on an individual path at an individual moment of decision, others had gone before me, and I was receiving the acknowledgment and welcome of a community of seekers. Marriage and death are other obvious moments of the need for such ritual, but what about the passing of an ordinary day? Stopping to acknowledge our progress, even in the midst of the mundane, has value.

I have begun an early morning practice of *pranayama* (yogic breathing exercises) and meditation that serve as anchors. They force me to pause, to reflect, before launching into the day's activities. As I breathe in sequences and patterns, I am acknowledging the value of this new day, my gratitude for the air that sustains me. As I come to silence, repeating a mantra or prayer, I am creating space and time apart from the hurly-burly that awaits me, giving importance to that very moment in time, discouraging myself from regrets of the past or worries of the future, simply acknowledging the present. The practice pulls me out of the particular into the universal and puts my life in perspective.

This is true as well of church on Sunday, of the liturgical landmarks of the Christian year, of New Year's Day, and of my birthday. Like Egeria's marking of the significance of her arrival at each destination on her itinerary, these occasions transform my life, rescue it from its quotidian existence, lift it from the ordinary to the extraordinary.

I love to set tables, and nearly every night of the summer, I head out into the garden to pick a bouquet. Its nature—the shape and color—changes endlessly from one day to the next. Cutting the flowers and arranging them in a vase for display gives me a chance to acknowledge the state of the garden and of each plant at the present moment. It transforms our dinner table as well, making it into a kind of household altar on which to recognize the passing of another day.

✿

As I look back at Egeria's pilgrimage, and as I long for personal reflection that might let me in on her evolving spiritual development, I am reminded that any journey—physical or otherwise—needs a series of destinations, a set of questions, that moves it along and governs choices along the way. For me, many such questions recur, drive me, and motivate and guide me as I read Christian history. These questions, I am learning, may never have answers, or their answers may change according to the time and place that they are posed.

I have searched, for example, for ways to take this strange and overwhelming new interest and integrate it into my daily life. I have wondered whether it will ever be possible for me—a woman who was raised in skepticism and doubt—to believe, to count myself among the faithful, and to profess the creeds that delineate their path. I wonder what it means to trust or to love God and what it would mean to say that God loves me. What would it be like to surrender to the will of God? I want to be a Christian, but I am so new that I don't yet know how to think about Christ, whether Christ represents a way of life on which to pattern my own, or whether Christ is a cosmic presence, a mythic source of transformation and transcendence. I want to grapple with the notion of sin, and I wonder whether I will ever be comfortable thinking of myself as a sinner. What is salvation? How do I get it, and do I care? Will I ever be able to use this language without worrying about rejection by my parents?

I want to know what is pulling me forward, what I am resisting, what I am afraid of. I want to know if the way will be easy, or if it will inevitably be full of pain. I want to know if it is possible to experience God directly and, if so, how to do it. I wonder if this new obsession will change my life, change what I do, the way I make decisions, the people I associate with. I wonder if it will change me.

The light lasts longer with every passing day of June. The warm rays of this ever present sun have given strength to my new plants. They are well established and launched now, well on the way to living out their individual destinies. This begins a cycle of growth for the residents of my garden and for me. I look forward to reflecting on our common progress and—like Egeria—recording the stages of the journey.

Saint Augustine and the Nature of Belief

High summer. The longest day is behind us. The sun has turned a corner, and from now on, the power of its light will slowly diminish as its distance from the earth begins to increase. The leaves of the trees have deepened from the bright, fresh green of spring to a darker, more mature shade. The flowers have begun to blossom in earnest, and the vegetables are beginning to replace their flowers with fruit. This ripening, this fruiting of midsummer, suggests some of the changes that I have begun to experience in midlife.

C. G. Jung wrote that he wished there were special colleges for forty-year-olds:

> Thoroughly unprepared we take the step into the afternoon of life; worse still, we take this step with the false assumption that our truths and ideals will serve us as hitherto. But we cannot live the afternoon of life according to the programme of life's morning; for what was great in the morning will be little at evening, and what in the morning was true will at evening have become a lie.

For me, the changes at midlife have not been subtle. Along with the disruption of leaving a job and facing an empty nest, I seem to have experienced a basic reordering of thought, a radical change in the very way I perceive the world. I feel as if I have been riding out an upheaval of mental tectonic plates and experiencing a shift from logical, analytical patterns of thought toward thinking that is more intuitive. Working in the garden has been a way of nurturing that sea change.

I have always loved a story about the work habits of Seymour Cray, the designer of supercomputers and founder of Cray Research. Whenever he experienced a mental block and was unable to figure out the next step in developing his latest circuitry, he would leave his computer, grab a shovel, and dig another few feet in a tunnel in his backyard. The tunnel went nowhere. It had no other purpose than just this: to force him out of the logical sequences of mathematical and scientific thought, to give the left brain a rest and enough creative space to permit the next breakthrough to come.

My garden works a little like Cray's tunnel. Of course, gardening has some analytical aspects: which flowers are tall and should go in the back of the border, which ones bloom early or late, what combinations of fertilizer are right. But for the most part, moving to the garden means losing myself in an activity that is physical but also intuitive, where the process of decision making seems to bypass the brain and flow from the heart.

In July, for example, I can begin to see where the spring planting went wrong. There is too much yellow in the perennial garden, too much white in the annual bed. The red dahlia is too big for its spot, the white one too small. I begin a process of editing: moving some things, pulling others out, replacing those with new plants. I don't consciously deliberate. I work as I've always imagined a painter would work, adding a dab of blue here, some yellow there, driven by an instinctive urge that emanates from the right side of my brain, not the left.

For me, the upheaval of midlife and the process of conversion have involved a shift in the balance of these two spheres of thought: a gradual diminishing of the role that pure reason and analysis have played in my life, and the emergence of a stronger intuitive mode.

As I was growing up, I was not aware that there were different orders of thought, different forms of truth. In school, for example, knowledge was knowledge. The studies of mathematics, geography, and history all seemed to involve a set of facts that needed to be understood and then committed to memory. For the most part, these facts concerned events, times, or places that I had not directly experienced; nonetheless, I had the impression that they were objectively true, and learning was a matter of storing their truth in my accumulated body of knowledge.

Because I had no exposure to religion at home, the story of Jesus was in a strange category. On the one hand, it had the earmarks of a fantastic tale, such as a virgin birth and miracles that just didn't happen in real life. On the other hand, it was reputed to be a true story and one that people believed, more like history than fiction. My parents acknowledged that Jesus was one of the greatest men that ever lived, but beyond that the story had no extraordinary power.

Belief, in my book, was related to truth. If I believed something, it was because the evidence was plain or the witnesses credible. I could believe that dinosaurs once roamed the earth or that Africa existed, because they were presented as well-documented facts. As far as I was concerned, the people who believed the Gospels were either stupid or kidding themselves.

The Confessions of Saint Augustine, written from 397 to 401 C.E., about the same time as Egeria's diary, reads at first as a poignant and scrupulous examination of conscience, in which the author goes back over his life, acknowledges his early preoccupation with lust and bodily pleasures, and recounts his eventual transition to a life of chastity and devotion to God. On closer reading, I found that the book chronicles a shift in the very nature of Augustine's thinking, a reordering of thought not unlike my own, from a bias toward logic and verifiability to a blossoming of the intuitive and another form of truth.

In *The Confessions,* Augustine wrote of his early attitude toward religion: "I held my heart back from positively accepting anything. . . . I wanted to be just as certain about things which I could not see as I was certain that seven and three make ten." Like me, Augustine of Hippo spent the first few decades of his adult life looking to logic and science for the answers to ultimate questions.

This brilliant student, who was the son of North African Berbers, left his hometown at age sixteen for Carthage to pursue his formal education. He wrote of his fascination with science, with Greek and Roman philosophy, and with the study of rhetoric. Although his mother was a fervent Christian and wished her son to be one as well, Augustine was more inclined to follow in his father's pagan footsteps.

Augustine was attracted to the Manichaeans, a sect who believed in a dualistic system that pitted the forces of good and evil against each other in the person of two great gods, one of light, the other of darkness. Augustine was lured by the Manichaean assertion that all their beliefs could be explained and proved by reasoning. After nearly ten years with this sect, Augustine finally met his hero, Faustus, their renowned apologist, and was surprised to find him unable to respond satisfactorily to questions of inconsistency between their texts and other books in regard to the movement of the sun, the moon, and the stars. That disappointment marked the beginning of Augustine's disillusionment with Manichaeism. When he left Carthage for Italy to further his career as a master of rhetoric, he had already opened himself to the possibility of religious alternatives. In Milan he met a Catholic bishop, Saint Ambrose, who was to play a key role in his conversion to Christianity. Augustine wrote of Ambrose in *The Confessions:*

> That man of God welcomed me as a father and, in his capacity of bishop, was kind enough to approve my coming there. I began to love him at first not as a teacher of the truth (for I had quite despaired of finding it in your Church) but simply as a man who was kind and generous to me. . . . As I opened my heart in order to recognize how eloquently he was speaking it occurred to me at the same time (though this idea came gradually) how truly he was speaking.

Augustine also began to see that his own years of rigorous analysis of the Scriptures had perhaps been misdirected energy. He said:

> I was happy when I heard Ambrose in his sermons, as I often did, recommend most emphatically to his congregation this text as a rule to go by: *The letter killeth, but the spirit giveth life.* So he would draw aside the veil of mystery and explain in a

spiritual sense the meanings of things which, if understood literally, appeared to be teaching what was wrong.

Under the guidance of Bishop Ambrose and another elderly priest, Simplicianus, Augustine spent two years working to free his mind from the limitations of materialism, to open his spirit to the possibility of unverifiable truths, and to turn his mind from sensual pleasures to the love of God. Like me, he often sought refuge and inspiration in the garden. One day he wrote, "To this garden the tumult in my heart had driven me, as to a place where no one could intervene." There, in desperation and confusion, he wrestled with the conflicting forces in his soul, the lure of the pleasures of the flesh against the promise of spiritual rewards. He threw himself on the ground and wept. Suddenly he heard a strange voice from nowhere repeating, "'Take it and read it.'" Augustine picked up a Bible he had brought with him and opened it, determined to honor the first passage he saw. He read the words of the Apostle Paul, urging him to turn his back on the ways of the flesh. With that, Augustine was finally able to yield to his own developing spiritual will and to adopt a new life entirely devoted to God.

After the scene in the garden, Augustine resigned from his teaching position. On the Saturday before Easter the following spring, Bishop Ambrose baptized him in the Catholic church, and Augustine's anxieties about his past disappeared:

> How deeply was I moved by the voices of your sweet singing Church! Those voices flowed into my ears and the truth was distilled into my heart, which overflowed with my passionate devotion. Tears ran from my eyes and happy I was in those tears.

In college, like Augustine, I fell in love with philosophy. I was immediately attracted to the weightiness of its questions: What is the good, and how do we make ethical judgments? How do we know what we know? What is the beautiful, and how do we make aesthetic observations? Is there free will? I loved the logic of it all, the way one assumption dovetailed with another, the way the conclusion flowed out of the assumptions, and the way one could "prove," through the cleverness of one's arguments, important statements about critical things. I enjoyed the lectures, the convoluted reading, and the late-night debates, and I eventually decided to be a philosophy major, devoting the better part of my last two years at Smith to the intricacies of the exercise of pure reason. When asked what I would "do" with such a major, I replied that it was teaching me how to think.

However, there are other ways to think—metaphorically, intuitively, creatively—and in the early decades of my adult life, I began to understand the importance of some of them. I read a lot, and most of what I read was fiction. I learned about time from Thomas Mann and memory from Marcel Proust. The novels of John Updike and Jane Smiley introduced me to the intricacies of marriage; those of Sue Miller and Mary Gordon to the vulnerabilities and pitfalls of motherhood. I loved the theater, and I learned that the works of Aeschylus or Shakespeare could illuminate aspects of my own life even in the strange language of another era, another culture. I loved music, and I discovered that listening to Brahms or Mahler turned me inside out, surprising me with the depths of emotional response they elicited. The arts stirred up my imagination, and I began to understand that the aptness and vividness of their images and metaphors were far more reliable vehicles of truth than the sequences of a philosophical argument.

It occurred to me in the years after I left my job at Dayton Hudson that perhaps the myths and metaphors imbedded in the sacred texts of religion could, like literature or theater, prove to be rich sources for insight and understanding. I wanted to mine the literature and liturgy of Christianity for such gems of truth, but, and here I hesitated every time, could I ever actually believe?

Like Augustine, I was lucky enough to find a mentor who has been essential to my spiritual progress. In July 1991, when I wrote the letter to the Episcopal bishop of Minnesota, I wasn't sure that the man I had met in the Denver airport ten years before would remember me, and I didn't really know what it was I wanted from him. I only knew that I had to talk to someone, but I knew no other members of the clergy. I had to move beyond books and begin to do something about it all. The bishop did remember me, and he agreed to meet with me in his office shortly thereafter.

He was excited about what I was experiencing. He appreciated the breadth of the influences on me. The one piece of advice that he gave me was "not to lead the horse into any one stall too soon, to play with my options, and to see where it all leads." He did not try to convince me of anything or persuade me to follow his path. I told him I was interested in becoming a Christian, but that I despaired of being required to recite statements of belief, things like the Nicene Creed. "Think of it as a song," he said, smiling, and he invited me to return in a month to let him know how it was all coming.

"Think of it as a song." This notion of linking liturgy to art was instantly powerful for me. It gave me permission to relax into it, to begin to hear the words as poetry, and to enter a church much as I did a concert hall or a theater. I learned that I could let the narrative stories, the phrases, and the images they evoked enter my consciousness unchallenged, let them shape my feelings and inform my intuitive response without applying tests of truth in a scientific or historical sense.

I signed up for confirmation classes at Saint Mark's Episcopal Cathedral in Minneapolis a couple of months after meeting with the bishop for the first time. I wasn't sure that this was the answer for me, but I knew I would learn enough from these encounters to see if it could work. At our first class, we received a book entitled *So You Think You're Not Religious*. Written by James R. Adams, an Episcopal priest from Washington, D.C., this text of our confirmation class stated that the word *creed* comes from the Latin *credo*. It is usually translated "I believe," but it literally means "to set the heart." The Nicene and Apostles' Creeds, which feature so prominently in the worship service, are not necessarily intended to bear witness to the objective truth of what they say, but rather to be a statement of choice, a recitation of what I as a Christian believe, the direction in which I have set my heart.

We were given another collection of essays entitled *What Is Anglicanism?* by Urban T. Holmes III. It told us that the Episcopal tradition that grew out of the Anglican church of England is characterized by "thinking with the left hand" (or right brain), thinking in a way that is "intuitive, analogical, metaphorical, symbolic and characteristic of poetry, art and music." The cathedral clergy who conducted the class were intelligent, witty, and open. I began to feel as if Saint Mark's was a church in which I could ground myself, a spiritual base from which I might continue to read and search according to my own schedule and inclination.

Augustine wrestled too with this question of the order of things:

> Grant me, O Lord, to know and understand which should
> come first, prayer or praise; or, indeed, whether knowledge
> should precede prayer. For how can one pray to you unless one
> knows you? . . . Or is it rather the case that we should pray
> to you in order that we may come to know you? But *how shall
> they call on him in whom they have not believed?*

I soon began to understand that I did not suddenly have to change
from an interested, curious seeker into a committed Christian that
knew exactly what she believed, but simply to set my heart in that
direction and let the process take care of itself.

On a cold November night just before Thanksgiving in 1991,
the members of my confirmation class—some in their twenties,
and others, like me, who had had a midlife change of heart—
gathered together in the front of the Saint Mark's sanctuary. They
had all come, united by then as a community of sorts, to bear
witness to the baptism of two of their own. Just minutes before, the
three members of the cathedral clergy, two men and a woman who
had by then become our friends, had been offering considerable wit
and wisdom in response to a "Quiz the Clergy" session, in which we
challenged them with our skepticism, our doubts.

Suddenly the clergy reappeared, robed in white, and the mood
changed. We gathered around the baptismal font, and together we
entered a different realm. We crossed over from the everyday to the
extraordinary, from the head to the heart. We lifted the prayer
books and recited together the ancient words, the poetry that for
hundreds of years has served to welcome people into the Episcopal
church. I stepped forward. "I baptize you in the name of the Father,
of the Son, and of the Holy Spirit." As I felt the warm water lap my
forehead, it was holy water. As I felt the shape of the cross being
traced in oil on my forehead, it was sealing me forever into this new
life I had chosen.

It was not necessary to listen too closely to the words, to test
them against my better judgment. It was enough to know that
tradition, myth, and the collective wisdom of the ages had said that
it was so.

We moved to a small chapel behind us for Communion. As I
knelt and took the wafer for the first time, I heard a voice pro-
nounce it the body of Christ, and it was. As I tipped the chalice to

my lips, I heard "the blood of Christ, the cup of salvation," and it was. As I stood up, the taste of wine still on my tongue, I savored the ritual, and I saw that this sacramental act was my testimony that I was there, body and soul, willing to suspend my analytical self and deliberately open myself to the Mystery. It was deeply satisfying, and I knew I would be back to relive that moment again and again. Saint Augustine spoke for me: "And I heard, as one hears things in the heart, and there was no longer any reason at all for me to doubt."

In the nearly two years since my baptism, I have learned that practice and ritual are the keys to belief. If I hear, over and over, Sunday after Sunday, month after month, "Thou shalt love thy neighbor as thyself," the words begin to sink into my bones, to recast my attitude, and to change the way I look at other people. If every single day I say, "Thine is the kingdom, the power, and the glory," I begin, ever so slowly, to believe it. The glory I am in the habit of seeking and the power I have always claimed begin to lose their grip on me. My orientation begins to shift. I am discovering that it is not necessary to be convinced in advance of the truth of the things one says in the act of worship. Rather, regular worship creates a context that sets the heart, shapes belief, and results in new patterns of behavior and action. It is there that truth resides.

The four weeks after midsummer are known in the Christian calendar as Saint John's Tide, the period that follows the celebration of the birth of John the Baptist. It is often overlooked in the stripped-down calendar of contemporary Christians, but it is very much in tune with the spirit of fecundity and growth that is so much a part of this season.

John the Baptist was sent to herald the coming of Christ. He preached fervently, calling for a change of heart in all who heard him, and he urged them to find new life through baptism in the River Jordan. It was John who baptized Jesus, thereby initiating Jesus' ministry. Thus, baptism, the recognition of a change of heart that ushers in new life, is what Saint John's Tide and midsummer are all about.

I enter a church now much as I enter the garden. It is a place where the intuitive—where imagination and spirit—reign supreme, where, as Seymour Cray did in his tunnel, I suspend my logical, analytical self. It is a place where—just as I use the whites, reds, and blues of midsummer flowers to create a tapestry of color—I use the words of the Scriptures, prayer, and creed to give me access to a new kind of truth, to inspire new understanding, and to give shape to a new life.

Seeking Balance
and the Rule of Saint Benedict

A delicate balance governs growth in the garden. In this northern part of the country, we have a short growing season, and the plants need just the right proportions of sun and shade, of daylight and darkness in order to reach their full potential. If these or other factors fall out of balance, the plants will not grow, or they will become slowed, leggy, pale, or languid. This summer, for example, we have had very heavy rains. In central Minnesota, we are lucky to have avoided serious floods, but many of the farmers' crops are ruined—the corn stunted by too much moisture and not enough sun, the spring wheat tainted with fungus. In my own garden, the tomatoes and snapdragons are way behind schedule, and the daylilies that border the swelling marsh are seriously threatened.

People too need balance to help them thrive. A human being is one unified organism with various aspects—body, mind, and spirit—each of which responds to specific kinds of nurturing and support. Our brief lives are like a short growing season. Establishing the right balance helps us reach our full potential.

Saint Benedict was in search of the right kind of balance when, toward the beginning of the sixth century, he composed his Rule for life in a monastery. Born into a distinguished Italian family, Benedict gave up his inheritance and abandoned his education early to dedicate his life to a search for God. He spent three years pursuing a life of solitude and asceticism, retreating in a cave at Subiaco. He worked to achieve a life of righteousness and virtue, fighting particularly hard against the tortures of lust. He finally triumphed, we are told by his biographer Gregory the Great, when—faced with an overwhelming temptation—he rolled naked in a patch of nettles. According to legend, the memory of the pain was enough to cure him of the lures of the flesh for the rest of his life. Rolling in nettles may have worked for Saint Benedict, but I have happened upon many a patch in my life as a gardener, and my hands have been subjected to their stinging treatment. Hideous as the experience may be, the memory of it fades fast, and I doubt that for me it would be enough to banish lustful musings for a lifetime!

Benedict's modeling of the virtuous life soon attracted others to follow him and try to learn for themselves the secrets that would eventually lead them to God. Benedict responded to this call to leadership and began forming his disciples into communities that eventually became twelve monasteries located throughout the Italian countryside. He wrote down his principles for the communities of monks, and this Rule of Saint Benedict has endured for over fourteen hundred years. The Rule serves not only as a guide for Benedictine monastic life but also as an inspiration to lay readers, who find guidance in his words that helps them lead satisfying, productive, and spiritual lives.

Saint Benedict's Rule and the monastic tradition he promoted are related to the fourth-century hermits who withdrew to live in caves and cells scattered throughout the Egyptian desert. The movement had received inspiration from the philosophy of Origen of Alexandria, a third-century theologian. Origen was among the first to write down the principles of the Christian life, which, for him, were rooted in asceticism and denial. Using the image of a ladder, Origen described the stages necessary to the attainment of salvation, sanctification, and union with God. With the decline of the Roman Empire at the end of the fourth century, and with the ensuing waves of invading barbarians, many Christians saw only futility in the pursuit of worldly goals and fled alone to the desert in a single-minded quest for God.

This desert tradition produced several great ascetic predecessors to Benedict: Antony the Great, who died in 396 and further developed Origen's principles; Pachomius, a contemporary of Antony who was the first to develop a community devoted to asceticism; and Basil of Caesarea, who articulated the importance of community and developed a framework for Christian sanctification—a life grounded in contemplation but lived in proximity to other hermits who could offer one another support for their separate paths.

Through the writings of these desert Christians, the notion of the communal religious life spread to the West: to Rome, where they inspired the fifth-century writings of Augustine, John Cassian, and others, and eventually throughout all of Europe.

⁂

Benedict begins his Rule with this admonition:

> Listen carefully, my son, to the master's instructions, and attend to them with the ear of your heart. This is advice from a father who loves you; welcome it, and faithfully put it into practice. . . . This message of mine is for you, then, if you are ready to give up your will, once and for all.

Benedict's Rule offers a concise, practical set of instructions grounded in common sense and love that promises sanctification for those who practice it.

The principles of the Rule are comprehensive, and they embrace all aspects of life in a monastery. Balance, I find, is an underlying concept that is consistently applied and is a key to appreciating the Rule as a guide both to Benedictine life and to life in the world outside the monastery. The Rule addresses balance as it applies to the very structure of the monks' time, balance between solitude and community, and between a life of contemplation and one of action. For example, the Rule says: "Idleness is an enemy of the soul. Therefore, the brothers should be occupied according to schedule in either manual labor or holy reading." A Benedictine day was carefully designed to exercise all dimensions of a person's human capacity. Periods of physical work, intellectual stimulation, and prayer alternated throughout the day and created a balanced lifestyle that encouraged each practitioner to become a whole person.

Time was set aside for manual labor, for the rigorous exercise of the body in doing physical tasks. Monasteries had specialties— farming or skilled craftsmanship—that they pursued in order to earn their livelihood, and each resident was expected to participate. "If conditions dictate that they labor in the fields (harvesting), they should not be grieved, for they are truly monks when they must live by manual labor."

Monks were expected to keep their mind growing, so they read both the Scriptures and books from the library, which the Rule dictated they "should read carefully cover to cover."

For Benedict's monks, periods of worship punctuated each day from beginning to end: "The prophet says: 'Seven times daily I have sung Your praises' (Ps. 119:164). We will cleave to this sacred number if we perform our monastic duties at Lauds, Prime, Tierce, Sext, None, Vespers and Compline." The residents of the monasteries rose before dawn and went to the chapel, where they chanted psalms and recited prayers prescribed by the Daily Office. Morning and afternoon activities were interrupted with similar services. Vespers were said in the evening, and Compline before retiring at night. Prayer and praise were constantly on their lips, the very passage of time marked by the order of psalm and scripture. This routine, followed faithfully day after day, allowed the monks to grow in all the dimensions of their life and aimed to produce human beings who were physically fit, mentally sharp, and spiritually alive.

Other forms of balance are built into Benedict's design for monastic life: the tension between solitude and community lies at its heart. The urge to escape the pressures and temptations of worldly life led to withdrawal and the solitary hermitage that have always been associated with Benedictine orders. Community, however, has been equally important to the development of the tradition. In his Rule, Benedict states that he wrote it for cenobites, "who are the best kind of monks." However, a large proportion of his text is devoted to coping with issues of community: leadership, discipline, and hierarchy, as well as qualities like humility, respect, obedience, and patience that allow community to work. Benedict believed that suppressing selfish impulses for the good of the whole was critical to the stability of such a community.

The prevalence of prayer in the life of a monk establishes a contemplative center from which all else flows. "It becomes the disciple to be silent and to listen," Benedict wrote, urging his followers to ground themselves in interior tranquility. Inevitably, though, the monks were also immersed in daily life, in the tasks that needed doing, in the service that gave meaning to their life in this world. There were students to teach, the scriptorium and its manuscripts to be copied, crafts to be made, guests to be tended to, the sick to be treated, cooking and cleaning to be accomplished. Clearly from the attention given to these tasks in the Rule, they were viewed as having as much importance as the periods of prayer with which they were interspersed. Contemplation and action complemented and supported each other. They were two sides of one coin, and it was in the balance between the two that wholeness could be attained.

I am a modern woman, a wife and a mother, and I doubt that I will ever live in a monastery. I fantasize occasionally about spending a week or more in a Benedictine retreat, but it is in my own life as it is now that I must apply Benedict's principles and look for their enduring value.

Ten years ago, my life was a frantic rat race, entirely out of balance. I worked from early morning to late afternoon and often brought home a bulging briefcase. With four children at home, I was entirely oriented outward—to my work, to my family. Always needed, always busy. There were no pauses in my existence. My life had no stillness, no balance.

As I read Benedict now, I see how far I have come in the last couple of years. I began with radical surgery: leaving a full-time job. I now see that this action allowed me the time and freedom to design a life with new priorities, one that would give more equal weight to the needs of body, mind, and spirit.

One by one, I began to build the missing pieces into my life. I started with the body, and it became my teacher. I tried several different yoga classes, and eventually discovered the system of yoga brought to the West by Indian practitioner B. K. S. Iyengar.

Iyengar yoga is rigorous and exacting, aiming to help students build strength and endurance in a series of time-tested postures. The teachers are scrupulously trained and well grounded in anatomy, and all class work combines the use of traditional Sanskrit names for the poses with detailed and anatomically correct instructions for doing them. I am naturally quite flexible, so my first attempts were promising. Soon I was hooked.

Paschimottanasana, a forward bend, for example, involves sitting on the floor, legs straight in front of me. I lean forward, arms outstretched toward my feet, head lowered until it nearly rests on my knees. At first, coming into a pose like this, I feel all sorts of twinges, pockets of resistance, and my mind bounces like a Ping-Pong ball from one part of my body to another. I remind myself of what needs to be done: knees contracted and pressed down until they nearly touch the floor; thighs tight; back extended; neck and head relaxed. Soon I find that all thoughts of my busy day have left me.

The concentration within, the attentiveness to my body, forces me to abandon anxiety, fears, plans, reminiscences, fantasies, and all the thoughts that normally come and go, keeping a mind tense, preoccupied, and attached to the world. Benedict's Rule did not include yoga, but this kind of Eastern discipline can be found in many Christian monasteries today.

In Benedict's time, physical labor was necessary for the monks to live. Many of us today have to build physical exercise into our lifestyle. Certainly a washing machine, a dryer, a dishwasher, and a vacuum cleaner make keeping up a house more button-pushing than back-breaking labor. Gardening, on the other hand, requires hauling tools, bending over and pulling weeds, coiling hoses, digging, clipping, and getting thick black dirt under one's nails. It has now become a regular and important part of my life. Gardening, yoga, and walking form the physical side of what I hope is a more balanced life.

Though I had used my mind in my professional life, I soon found that I craved intellectual activity at a deeper level. I was active in the independent school that my son attended, and one day we parents were invited to visit a class. I chose sophomore English, taught by Mrs. Johnson, a teacher that I had had myself when I was a student there twenty years earlier. They were reading poetry, and she was making a valiant effort to get them to see the metaphors in a love poem. I remember the poet's image of crossing a lake to visit his lover, the "pushing prow of the boat" cutting insistently through the water. As I looked around the room at the ten or twelve adolescents in the class, I realized that not one of them (all of whom must surely have been privately obsessed with notions of sexual prowess) understood or saw the metaphor. The teacher's gentle hints were in vain. At that moment, I thought to myself: What a waste! It is I, not they, who should be studying! I have lived; at my age, I have something to bring to the table.

Until then I had always rejected thoughts of graduate school, assuming that such activity needed to be justified by career advancement or a job change. Suddenly I wanted to study again for the sheer exercise of intellect, to see if I could still use my mind. The master's in liberal studies program was the result. In finding balance, I would always need to make study a part of my life.

Finally, though we lead lives that are often as regulated as the days in a monastery, our schedules rarely provide for the exercise of spiritual muscles. The transcendent must rely, it seems, on catching us by surprise: a sunset, a strain of music, a poignant turn in a relationship. At those moments, we stop to acknowledge the presence of Spirit. We are lifted briefly out of the ordinary—we vibrate, we shine—but the thought of working those moments purposefully into our days or weeks is increasingly rare. I wanted to integrate Spirit into my life too.

Going to church once a week was an obvious beginning. I am still fascinated by it. I love the sacred music and the Gothic, soaring spaces of Saint Mark's Cathedral. The liturgy and the readings from the Scriptures have not yet become routine for me. Each week I discover a word here, a phrase there that sink into my consciousness in new ways, that pique my interest or spark my imagination. Going to church is pure pleasure, and I look forward to it every week.

I realized early on in this process, though, that I needed and wanted some kind of spiritual practice on a more frequent basis. Benedict with his "seven times daily" was too extreme for me, but so many of the spiritual writers I had read about and come to respect benefited from daily prayer or meditation that I knew I wanted to try to establish such a regular practice.

I took a series of classes in meditation at the local branch of the Himalayan Institute. Though I tried for several weeks to repeat a mantra for twenty minutes each afternoon, as I was taught, I found that my mind wandered hopelessly and my legs went to sleep. I soon gave up. I bought a book of inspirational phrases for each day of the month, but so many were sentimental or out of sync with my own state of mind that I abandoned that too.

But at one point, somehow, something changed. I had really enjoyed my most recent eight-week *pranayama* class, and when it ended, I missed it. I decided to try getting up just twenty minutes earlier each morning to practice. There was something almost sensually rewarding about crawling out of bed at sunrise when the rest of the house was still asleep, something exciting about being so alone. The world hadn't yet taken on its everyday, ordinary look. The light was mysterious; the birds were the only sound makers I heard.

I practiced the breathing patterns faithfully. They made me feel better physically, and the concentration they required disciplined my mind, helped calm the racing thoughts. After a few months, I found that when I had finished the *pranayama* exercises, I was so centered, so focused, that I wanted to continue to enjoy that state for a while longer. I had read a book called *Meditation,* by Eknath Eswaren, that suggested repeating the Saint Francis prayer very slowly over and over. Whereas a single one-word mantra had never worked for me, this slow, deliberate repeating of the longer prayer allowed me to stay focused on the task at hand. Gradually I began building that into my daily routine, and soon I was getting up even earlier to make it possible.

It is hard for me to believe, but it has been nearly two years now since I began this practice. Of course, I have days when I can't concentrate; my mind races; I am anxious and obsessed with fantasies. For the most part, though, it works reasonably well, and I find I need and look forward to these sessions more and more. This is a long way from performing the Daily Office like Benedict's monks, but there is no question that I am beginning to make prayer a priority.

The tensions between solitude and community and between contemplation and action in my life are a constant challenge. Now that I have more flexibility in my work life, there should be no excuse for letting them get out of balance. I find it nearly impossible nonetheless. In our world outside a monastery, it is not acceptable to turn down a request for our time because we need to be alone or have to spend time in meditation. I am a natural extrovert. I need people and crave company, but my lifelong habits of scheduling myself so tightly and staying so busy are beginning to wear me down and leave me longing for a different pace.

My life is radically different than it was ten years ago. It is moving closer to one that offers the kind of balance Saint Benedict wanted for his monks. But there are ways in which Saint Benedict and I will never meet, aspects of his Rule that, while appropriate for the monastery, are at odds with the kind of balance I am seeking.

Benedict must have known, for example, that the survival of the human race depends on procreation. Celibacy could not have been for everyone. The Rule warns the monks "not to succumb to the desires of the flesh." For them, lustful urges were a distraction from their intended focus on the path to God. My sexual relationship with my husband is a sacramental expression of marital commitment as well as an important outlet for physical desire. I find mystery and transcendence as well to be very much present in our physical intimacy.

The Rule calls for an evenhandedness and independence among the monks that seems to discourage intimate friendships. Perhaps, in monastic communal life, close alliances threatened to upset group dynamics, to create jealousies or favoritism. Perhaps intimacy was reserved for the relationship with God. I need the depth of interchange that love affords, whether it is with my husband or with good friends. Close friendships help me understand myself, give me support, and give me a community that our living in separate nuclear families does not provide. I have no assigned confessor—as I would in a monastery, where the confessor-confesee relationship is institutionalized—but my best friends offer me a means to unburden myself on occasion. Marriage brings me constant companionship, unconditional love, and builds the bonds of family that are necessary to raise children.

Getting the balance exactly right is difficult. For me, and for most of us who live in the world, a monastic Rule can only suggest guidelines and provide inspiration for change. It is designed for men and women who have dedicated their life to a particular intense form of spiritual devotion. Many different configurations of contemplation and action, of solitude and community, of occupations for the body, mind, and spirit will work. I look at my garden in this crazy year of too much rain, and I see, above all, resilience. The truth is, most things have survived. I never thought I would find any potatoes in the heavy clay that the soil has become, but they are there. The daylilies bloomed as profusely, it seemed, as any other year.

The weight will no doubt shift over time from one aspect of my life to another, but I know now when balance isn't there, and I doubt that I will ever go back to the kind of life I led ten years ago. Maybe, when I feel the need to reflect on this once again, I will find a way to spend a week or so in a Benedictine monastery.

SEPTEMBER

Out of Death, New Life: Julian of Norwich

The autumnal equinox is upon us: the days and nights are of equal length; light and darkness are poised in perfect balance against each other. In September, we live with contradictions like this, with the push and pull of opposites. High noon looks and feels like summer. The sun is strong, the air is warm, and the landscape is still lush and green. As the day wears on, though, it is clear that change is in the offing. As the sun nears the horizon, there is a nip in the air, and by seven o'clock, it is so dark that we need candles on the dinner table.

All around me, if I look closely, I see evidence of the paradox that is autumn: the simultaneous appearance of ripeness and decay. My potato plants are yellow and beginning to wither, but if I dig down under them with a shovel and turn over the earth, I find nestled among their roots clusters of firm, fleshy potatoes that boil up flaky and tender. Ripe red tomatoes hang from vines that are browning around the edges and sagging, spent from carrying the weight of their bounty. The daylilies are nearly finished blooming, but at the ends of many of the blackened, brittle stems are swollen pods containing the seeds of new life. The maples glow red here and there, as if a match has been tentatively touched to their branches, a prophecy of the flames that in a few short weeks will consume the life of summer. The oak trees are offering up a bumper crop of acorns that will see our hoarding chipmunks through the long, cold winter.

This fading away I see everywhere in the landscape and in the garden is accompanied by a harvest that offers sustenance and the promise of regeneration. Autumn is a living parable. Like the story of Jesus' death and Resurrection, it is a manifestation of paradox but ultimately a message of hope. This same kind of story finds expression in *Showings*, Julian of Norwich's late-fourteenth-century account of her sixteen visions, or revelations. The lessons of *Showings* find particular resonance at this time of year.

There is a gap of over eight hundred years between Benedict's Rule and Julian of Norwich's *Showings*. In that period, the Celtic church flowered in Ireland, the monastic movement grew and diversified in Europe, and the scholastic theological tradition grew up in the great universities with the likes of Thomas Aquinas. Julian represents for me, however, an important landmark: her book is the first ever written in English by a woman.

Julian of Norwich herself is something of a mystery. We know that she was born in 1342, but we do not know where. We do not know who her family was or anything about her early years. From her book, we can surmise that she entered a religious order when she was still quite young. Much of her adult life was lived as a solitary anchorite, enclosed in a cell across from a house of Augustinian friars in Norwich, England. The word *anchorite* comes from a Greek word meaning "to retire." As such, Julian continued the tradition of the early Christian anchorites who withdrew to desert cells for solitude and the opportunity for undistracted prayer. Today, we "retreat" for brief periods to find spiritual renewal; in Julian's case, "retreat" was a lifelong commitment.

As a young woman, Julian had prayed earnestly that she might be allowed to understand Christ's Passion by suffering herself. She prayed that she might be granted several wounds and an illness that would be so severe that she and everyone else would believe she was dying. In May of 1373, at the age of thirty, her wish was granted: "God sent me a bodily sickness in which I lay for three days and three nights; and on the fourth night I received all the rites of the Holy Church, and did not expect to live until day."

Indeed, Julian was convinced that she was dying, and she fixed her eyes on a crucifix that was held in front of her by the priest who had been called to her bedside. Gradually the crucifix seemed to come alive, and red blood began trickling down Christ's face from under his crown of thorns, "all hot, flowing freely and copiously, a living stream." This was the first of a series of sixteen showings, or visions, in which Julian encountered vivid mystical experiences. She participated bodily in Jesus' suffering upon the cross, and through that suffering she received spiritual insights that she wrote down for posterity: "Everything that I say about myself I mean to apply to all my fellow Christians, for I am taught that this is what our Lord intends in this spiritual revelation."

Julian's revelations were recorded twice: once shortly after she experienced her visions, and again, in an expanded version, some twenty years later. This "long text" benefits from years of reflection and inward instruction, and adds depth to the bare outline of the shorter version.

Julian takes us with her through her revelations, painfully and dramatically, one by one. We proceed from the dripping crown of thorns to a vision of Jesus' body bleeding profusely, of the wounds that pierce his tender flesh. We watch as Jesus nears death, as the vitality and freshness are drained from his body, as he withers and dries and thirsts on the cross, and we feel all his pains with him. The devil appears to Julian as well, the fiend "with his heat and his stench." Julian records vivid images of fear, sin, weakness, and brokenness.

These are painful revelations, but woven in with them, alternating with these visions of despair, are episodes in which Julian receives messages of bliss, triumph, and hope: "And suddenly, as I looked at the same cross, he changed to an appearance of joy. The change in his appearance changed mine, and I was as glad and joyful as I could possibly be." She describes this joyful Christ as "glad and merry." She talks with him in his glory and receives assurances of love.

Another vision, of a small hazelnut, reminds Julian that God is the Creator, the Lover, and the Protector of life, that "everything which he has made . . . is great and lovely and bountiful and good." She experiences Mary as mother in her delight and love and pride, and ultimately these maternal meditations coalesce into a sense of Christ Jesus, and ultimately of God, as Mother: "To the property of motherhood belong nature, love, wisdom and knowledge, and this is God."

In her visions of heaven, of rapture, of bliss, like a recurring leitmotiv in a piece of music, Julian repeats her pronouncements of hope again and again: that in spite of all the pain, the sin and suffering, God in God's compassion will triumph, and "all will be well, and all will be well."

What a strange work this is for a twentieth-century reader like me! At first I resisted any identification with Julian's words. Her melodramatic visions and her medieval penchant for macabre detail left me cold, and I felt no connection with her experience. As I spent more time with the work, though, I began to see some patterns and to learn from them.

Through the ups and downs of Julian's dramatic and often unpleasant series of revelations and reflections, we come to understand that a dialectical rhythm underlies life on earth. We cannot experience happiness unless we have known pain. Hope derives much of its meaning from despair; life does not exist without death. Each one of these concepts or qualities flows out of the other and derives its very meaning from that which precedes it. As we live, caught up in one experience or the other, we appear at some times to be hopelessly doomed, at others to be ultimately victorious. These are fleeting impressions, depending for their very definition on their opposing states.

Julian wrestled particularly with the issue of sin and forgiveness: why, if God is omnipotent and omniscient, were sin and suffering permitted in the first place? She carried on with God a lengthy dialog on this subject that takes up over thirty chapters of the eighty-six in the long text, and her conclusion can be summed up in one word: *compassion*. Sin, she says, arises not from wickedness but from human ignorance and naivete. Sin leads to self-knowledge and a quest for God. Though we suffer from the consequences of our sins, God is not wrathful but compassionate, and we will ultimately realize our reward. The *changeability* in this life will lead to eternal resolution, to *bliss* in transcendent unity. God's purposes are mysterious and hidden from us, but God has the power to resolve the contradictions that confound us now.

Christ becomes for Julian and for us a symbol of unity, of transcending apparently irreconcilable opposites. As he accepted death on earth to attain eternal life, as he suffered from the sins of humans in order to redeem them, so must we come to understand that in embracing both sides of any equation we find truth. "[Christ] taught that I should contemplate the glorious atonement," says Julian. It is in comprehending this "at-one-ment," this act of integration and transcendence, that we experience the meaning of the cross.

As I read *Showings* for the second time, it occurred to me that my own life, in one striking episode in particular, was an echo of Julian's. At about the same age she was when she contracted her mortal disease, I underwent my painful divorce, and it turned my life upside down. Like Julian, I was led into a series of important revelations.

When my husband announced that he was leaving, I was devastated. This was a "sickness" that loomed as large for me as Julian's life-threatening illness. I couldn't eat, couldn't sleep, and my world went black. I was convinced that I would never find another husband, another lover. I tortured myself with visions of empty Sunday mornings and lonely Saturday nights. I imagined that my son would never have a man in his everyday life, would never know a "normal" Christmas. In my mind, I cataloged household tasks I could not handle, financial burdens I could not bear. Though I never really thought, like Julian, that I wanted to die, I had lost much of what I had been living for.

This experience of pain and these agonizing visions were entirely new to me. Unlike Julian, I had never prayed for them, but like her, I gradually came to accept them. I had begun by fighting, by assuming that I could control the outcome of it all. Eventually I saw that I had no alternative but to give up, to yield to the inevitable, and even to begin to take responsibility for what had happened. For Julian, this acceptance was of death itself: "And I understood by my reason and the sensation of my pains that I should die; and with all the will of my heart I assented to be wholly as was God's will."

For me, acceptance was not of death itself, but of the death of a marriage. First, I came gradually to see that I bore a substantial portion of the blame. I had been insensitive to my husband's needs.

I had been selfish, so focused on myself and the way I wanted our lives to go that I hadn't really listened, hadn't been willing to compromise on little things, wasn't accustomed to seeking a middle ground. This "sin" on my part, as Julian said, did not stem from evil or deliberate wickedness, but from a lack of self-understanding, a very human ignorance, naivete, and willfulness. Though I had finally begun to understand the dynamics that had eroded our relationship, it was too late for my husband to change his mind. The marriage was over.

Slowly, I picked up the pieces. I began to earn my own money and to discover time for myself. I had a fireplace, and I used it. When the wind whined, and I could feel the draft coming up from under my living room window, I would wrap myself in a blanket and get up only to prod the embers in the fireplace grate that had originally been for coal. When there were no voices to fill the silence, I turned to music, and the sounds of Bach, Mozart, and Mahler pulled me out of the loneliness and delivered me into moments of bliss. I lost myself in books, and, for the first time in my life, I had the time to choose an author and read all of his or her books, one after another.

There was still pain. There was the loss of companionship and love. I had to learn to go to parties alone, to suffer the curiosity and well-meaning sympathy of my friends. I still experienced moments of anger, grief, and fear. Phases of suffering and joy alternated like an ascending spiral, leading me steadily up and out of the darkness.

> And then again I felt the pain, and then afterwards the delight and the joy, now the one and now the other, again and again.
> . . . Therefore it is not God's will that when we feel pain we should pursue it in sorrow and mourning for it, but that suddenly we should pass it over, and preserve ourselves in the endless delight which is God.

Looking back nearly twenty years later, this agonizing period was clearly one of the most important in my life. For the first time, I understood what it means to suffer. My own experience opened my eyes to the pain that was all around me. My friends began to talk freely with me, to reveal their own troubles and problems, to sense that I could empathize and would understand. Out of this very state of isolation, separateness, and loneliness grew a new capacity for relationships and for being in community.

I had originally been afraid for my son and the damage this divorce would do to him, but I came to believe that there was value for him in growing up with an understanding that life does not always turn out the way we hope, that there is disappointment and setback in every story. What I feared would be a weakness in his upbringing has created strength and realism that will serve him well in his own life.

The center of gravity shifted for me during those years, and it would never go back. I learned to think of myself as a whole person, responsible for myself. Even though I have remarried, I have never lost that new frame of reference. I am part of a partnership, one that I value and love and choose—every day—to stay in. But I know that if something happens and it falls apart, it will not be the end of the world. I know now that I can survive the pain and grow from it. That knowledge is good for a marriage and makes it stronger. It is my attitude of independence that makes our inter-dependence possible and able to endure.

Suffering and bliss, loneliness and community, weakness and strength, independence and interdependence: each of these states grows out of and is, to some degree, defined by the other. It is by embracing both sides, by receiving God's grace in all its forms, that we ultimately find truth.

Still, Julian's story is not my story. I can't imagine praying for suffering, even though I have learned it can be a valuable source of growth. I believe that I will have a different attitude next time I face real pain. I will know I can recover, and I will examine it more closely to discover what it is trying to teach me. I hope I will receive it rather than fight it, and I am no longer naive enough to think life is possible without it.

Julian's graphic images are not my images either. I am still a long way from a Christocentric spirituality like hers that identifies with Jesus, that merges her story with his. I am beginning to under-stand the dynamics of the cross and to see the patterns of death and resurrection in my own life, but not to yearn to share the humanity of Jesus' Passion with him.

۞

The vestments and altar cloths at Saint Mark's this month are, like the landscape that surrounds me, still green. They symbolize life and growth, the steady and inexorable spread of early Christianity through the work of the Holy Spirit. But on top of the green background, like the Minnesota trees touched with brilliant color, they are shot through with red and gold designs suggesting flames—echoes of Pentecost's tongues of fire, which proclaimed the word, which consumed the old laws and rules, and, in a simultaneous burst of energy, offered up out of the ashes a whole new way of life, one that demonstrates over and over the truth that rises from contradiction and paradox.

One of my favorite fall rituals is to clip some of the bittersweet vines that grow near our house. As the leaves wither and die back, they leave bright yellow capsules whose casings burst open when ripe to reveal scarlet berries inside. The presence of these exotic twisted stems in a vase in the house embody—by their very name—the essence of autumn: the bitterness of regret at the withering and dying of summer's leaves and flowers, but also the sweet promise of new life in the berries, the nuts, and the seeds that swell in their wake.

Julian's visions too are bittersweet. They are full of pain but also of hope. They suggest that just as fruit inevitably follows flower, suffering will eventually yield to joy. But Julian's positive message goes further than that. It says that truth lies not so much in the alternating patterns of pain and pleasure, of sin and forgiveness, but in the necessary embrace of both. We will find the resolution of paradox, she says, in welcoming the grace of a compassionate God and in transcendence through Christ of all opposites into eternal wholeness and unity. In the end, "all will be well, and all will be well, and every kind of thing will be well."

Letting Go: Meister Eckhart

Almost overnight the blazing canopy overhead has drifted down and settled into a crackling carpet of dry leaves. How easily this has been accomplished! The trees seem to surrender their leaves without resistance, yielding to the passing of a season. I wish that I could learn to live like that, to relax my grip on life, to become more receptive and less concerned with control.

With the shortening days of autumn and the onset of darkness, my spirit is beginning to turn inward. Whereas the sunlight of summer drew me into the world, this new chill in the air and the falling leaves are calming me down and inviting me to hold the world a little more loosely.

Autumn is a natural reflection of the spiritual path known as the *Via Negativa*. It is the path of inwardness, of stillness, of release, of letting go. As I seek wholeness and try to balance my own natural tendencies to control, to extroversion and activity, I am attracted to the *Via Negativa*. Meister Eckhart, a German mystic, has been a source of support and inspiration for me. I like the way he articulates the nature of God. He has reinforced my instinctive approach to prayer, and he has helped me bring balance to my life by encouraging me to let go.

As Huston Smith wrote in his preface to a collection of Eckhart's sermons and treatises: "Like prisoners, we had been straining at our bars, hoping for a sliver of light. [Eckhart] spins us around and shows us that the door behind us is wide open."

Eckhart was born in the second half of the thirteenth century into a turbulent period in European history, one of spiritual ferment and a proliferation of alternative forms of religious expression. The power of the papacy was under attack from all sides. Opulence, greed, and corruption among the clergy were disillusioning the populace and eroding their respect for the church. This created an atmosphere in which people were seeking a direct relationship with God and turning inward for spiritual satisfaction. The Rhineland Valley was a veritable breeding ground for mystics, including Meister Eckhart's immediate predecessors Hildegard of Bingen and Mechtild of Magdeburg.

We know little about Eckhart's youth and can only guess that he entered the Dominican order at about the age of sixteen. He was ordained to the priesthood and spent years studying alternately in Paris and in Cologne. In 1302, he completed his magisterial studies in theology in Paris and was forever after known as Meister, or Master, Eckhart. He eventually ended up at Strasburg as a professor of theology and, though he was a teacher and a scholar, his energy began to shift to preaching, the ministry that was to consume him for the rest of his life. Tonsured and robed in the traditional garb of the Dominican order, the Meister traveled widely among the monasteries and houses of contemplative sisters in the Rhineland Valley. He developed a devoted following of nuns, monks, and friars for whom he provided inspiration and spiritual direction.

Though the Meister offered an inspired alternative for those on the receiving end of his ministry, his teaching was perceived as a threat to the established church. Eckhart's message that people could achieve a unity with God "so intimate that there would be no need for kneeling and bowing, no room for a priest in between" was not ignored. In 1326, the archbishop of Cologne culled 150 propositions from the Meister's works and attacked their orthodoxy. Eckhart was accused of heretical notions such as pantheism (claiming human equality with God), and of promoting independence from ecclesiastical authority. He was forced to mount a lengthy defense, in which he maintained his papal allegiance until the end, arguing that he never intended heresy and offering to recant anything judged to be potentially heretical. He lost and, though he tried to appeal, was condemned by Pope John XXII in a 1329 papal bull, issued a year after Eckhart's death.

The teachings of Meister Eckhart, which have come down to us mostly through records of his sermons, are complex. His style is often repetitive and confusing. I have had to consult several secondary sources to help clarify his thought for myself and to give coherence to the many individual sermons I have read.

Eckhart's ideas focus generally on personal transformation: the process that leads a seeker from his or her fallen state back to unity with God. Human beings, as they were originally created, were aware of their divine source in the Creator. With the Fall, with Adam and Eve's sin, humankind lost its innocence and direct awareness of God, though individuals still keep an essential connection to the divine. Robert K. C. Forman explains Eckhart's belief: "[Humanity] retains an inner unity with God at the deepest level, in the 'ground.' 'In the ground of the soul . . . God's ground and the soul's ground are one ground.' There God 'indwells.'"

Thus, fallen human beings are creatures divided. Their conscious mind is caught up in the whirl of existence. Emotions and desires captivate them. The pleasures of fame and power, of sex and money—the world of material things—seduce and enslave them. Work, family, friends, and religious practices distract them and ensnare them in the web of illusion that is life on earth and leave them unaware of their deep inner connection to the divine.

Eckhart advocates a process of detachment to lead people out of this creaturely prison to the rediscovery of God: "Keep this in mind: to be full of things is to be empty of God, while to be empty of things is to be full of God." In other words, blessed are the poor in spirit, and for Eckhart true spiritual poverty consists in freeing the mind of every single creaturely notion, including even thoughts about God. For the human mind to hold the notion of God, it must imbue God with characteristics or qualities, but for Eckhart, "God is nameless, for no one can know or articulate anything about God." God, for Eckhart, is a "being beyond being and a nothingness beyond being." So "we must stop projecting onto God our notions of who God is." How then should we love God? Absolutely mindlessly, says Eckhart: "For if you love God as he is God or mind or person or picture, all that must be dropped. . . . You should love him as he is, a not-God, not-person, not-image—even more, as he is a pure, clear, One, separate from all twoness." This is true spiritual poverty: the creation of an inner stillness, a darkness from which all distractions and desires are removed, a spiritual vacuum that allows the One to fill the space.

Letting go is a key to detachment for Eckhart. The human will, a determined and forceful instrument of control, can only be an obstacle on the path to God. The concepts of searching, of actively seeking, of trying are all futile, "for it is when you do not seek him that you find him," says Eckhart. Human beings can only let go of their attachments and allow God to fill the space that is created. By giving up the things our ego clings to—the world, even notions of self and God—we arrive at our destination, identification with the One: "Let your own 'being you' sink into and flow away into God's 'being God.' Then your 'you' and God's, 'his,' will become so completely one 'my' that you will eternally know with him his changeless existence and his nameless nothingness." This is the point of total detachment for Eckhart. At first, it is achieved temporarily, it is a mere glimpse of the eternal.

Eventually, however, through a slow process of personal discovery and steady evolution, a seeker can gradually achieve the Birth of the Word in the Soul. This is a state in which the awareness of the eternal is constantly maintained. One's identity with God is so complete that there is reflexive awareness: one is at once the seer and the seen. One sees oneself at work in the world, but knows that one shares identity with the Source of it all. Persons know themselves to be expanded and live rather like the Janus figure: one face turned toward ordinary life and the world, the other turned toward God, eternally aware of itself as infinitely expanded.

For Eckhart, the final stage achievable on earth is the breakthrough of the soul to the Godhead. The perspective that was achieved in the birth begins to pervade one's actions and one's being in the world. One actually identifies with God:

> In the breakthrough . . . where I stand free of my own will and of the will of God and of all his works and of God himself, there I am above all creatures and am neither God nor creature. . . . For in this breakthrough I discover that God and I are one. There I am what I was.

This sense of unity, of total identification with every person and every thing, becomes for Eckhart very much a philosophy of action in the end. One is aware of being intimately connected at the core to every other being—of meeting one's self, so to speak, in every encounter. One participates fully in the world, but one is motivated by God and moves only toward God.

This spiritual quest of mine seems above all to be a search for God. It flows from a need, a longing for the presence of the infinite in my life. I have come a long way just to be able to use the word *God* with some comfort. As I was growing up, I was told over and over that of all the misguided teachings of the Judeo-Christian tradition, the worst was the sentimental notion of an anthropomorphic God, the need that Christians and Jews had to make God into a person in order to understand God. Those admonitions have stayed with me, and I still feel uneasy with prayer that takes the form of an imagined dialog with a being that is like the other beings I know. I resist characterizations of God as wrathful, punitive, patient, forgiving, empathetic, and even loving.

I was excited to find in the writings of Meister Eckhart a God that was without name, without boundaries, without qualities, a "pure, form-free being of divine unity." I had discovered God myself not through positing an image or a theory or by projection, but rather through a process of negation. By coming to stillness, by creating a sort of mental vacuum, I came home to an underlying, all-embracing Presence that could not be contained or defined. This God is what is left when everything we know or can name is taken away. This God is pure mystery, without recognizable form or character, simply and at once both everything and no-thing.

Prayer, then, for me becomes a need to create a state of pure receptivity that is formless in its own way. It means becoming nothing myself: no thoughts, no memories, no fantasies—just silence, darkness, and a kind of turning inside out that allows me to touch and be filled with that infinite One. That is most difficult to do, and I struggle constantly with how to achieve it. Meister Eckhart even warns against slavish devotion to any particular technique: "You should not restrict yourself to any method, for God is not in any one kind of devotion, neither in this nor in that. Those who receive God thus, do him wrong. They receive the method and not God."

As human beings, we are who we are, trapped in our limited form and with our limited understanding. Of necessity, we have created paradigms of the imagination—myths, stories, and rituals—that allow us to deal with the infinite in a metaphorical way. I am learning, despite my upbringing, that there is truth to be found in those myths and stories, and that the path of formal worship and traditional Scriptures and liturgy is not a misguided delusion, but a rich and effective way to fill our life with a taste of the Unknowable. Eckhart commonly quoted the Scriptures in his sermons, so for him "method" must not have included metaphor.

The spiritual life, I am discovering, is not limited to the sphere of discussion about God. Just as the sacred extends beyond the boundaries of the church and onto the ground of our everyday life, so the attitudes we adopt are meant to carry over into the world of the profane. Through letting go, Meister Eckhart tells us, we are able to discover God. Only by giving up trying, searching, and seeking do we finally reach our goal. As the Gospel says, "'For those who want to save their life will lose it, and those who lose their life for my sake will find it'" (Matthew 16:25). If there is one thing that I need most, one aspect of transformation that I hope for in this spiritual adventure, it is this: that I can learn to let go.

I have, of course, been shown the way on many occasions. My divorce was a case in point. I hung on for dear life, tried everything to keep my husband and to stop the inevitable course of things, but only when I finally let him go could I move on, grow in new ways, and receive the gifts of independence, self-reliance, new love, and new life. At Dayton Hudson too, I hung on, thinking that a higher salary, a new title, and a bigger office were the kind of growth I needed. Only when I gave up my job altogether did I find what I was really seeking: a new way of life that allowed me to discover my true interests and vocation.

Angus also has been a teacher. Before I began seeing him, I had spent a year and a half in love with a witty and handsome man. When I began seeing Angus, this man had just left Minnesota for Washington, D.C., to work for the newly elected vice-president in the new Democratic administration. Our relationship hadn't ended exactly, but it had been interrupted by his leaving town. I began keeping company with Angus in the interim. One day, just after Christmas, I got a call from my friend in Washington, inviting me to fly out for the inauguration. I would stay with him, of course. We would ride in the inaugural motorcade and attend all the festivities of the weekend. By that time, I was more than a little interested in Angus, and the thought that this might hurt him was much on my mind. I told him about the invitation.

"Just go," he said. "It's the chance of a lifetime, and besides— if I have to put a rope around your neck, it will never work anyway." I remember being stunned by his response. I wrote him a letter from the plane as I flew to Washington, telling him how like a giant magnet it was, this freedom he was giving me. Angus let me go, and I hurried back a week later, ready to marry him.

My son, Phil, is also a teacher, but I am a reluctant student. He is my only child, and when he was born, it was as if I experienced a radical and profound shift—the whole tenor of life changed. Suddenly the horror of what I had at stake was clear to me. This son I had and the vulnerability he brought me was a gaping hole in my armor, but it was also to be the hole through which life's most satisfying rewards would pass. My instinct though, in the face of it, was to hold on tight, to put a psychic rope around his neck, and to try to control his fate and mine.

Every year, it seemed, he begged to be allowed to participate in a summer activity that terrified me: a bicycle tour of Colorado in eighth grade, a monthlong alpine climbing program at fifteen, another climb alone with a guide the next year. As a high school senior, he, and his best friend, bicycled from Minneapolis to California. Each time, I agonized, I cried, but I said yes. Each time, I was sure this was it, but each time, he came back, stronger and more independent than he had left. By the time he was ready for college, I had had so much practice that I was ready to let him go.

I am a golfer and a tennis player, and I have learned over the years that the times I play best are the times when I am not focused on the score. When I give up on the outcome, when I let go of winning, I play with freedom and confidence and do much better as a result. Still, I am a woman of control. If I am the chair of a committee, I am much too likely to make a few calls before the meeting to make sure that things go the way I want them to. I have no doubt that my approach has in many cases led to a poorer outcome than the one that might have emerged from a free and open discussion.

Letting go is an attitude of acceptance, of reverence, of respect for the autonomy of things and other people. It stems from openness, and it invites surprise and results that are better than I might have achieved on my own. It is an attitude of detachment that says that there are more important things than achieving my own personal objectives. It is also an attitude of trust that relies on and believes in my neighbor as an extension of myself. It is an attitude that understands the limitations of the human will, that is open and ready to receive, to recognize, and to welcome the power of God's grace.

Letting go, or detachment, does not mean giving up being organized or working hard. It is not the same as disengagement. It is a matter of moving beyond the ego and its selfish needs to a state of compassion, an expanded consciousness in which I see myself as an integral part of the whole, one with "the other."

This has been a remarkable month, full of warm days and blue skies. I have watched the very last green tree, a linden right in front of our house, turn yellow overnight. As the wind picks up in the next day or two, bringing in the cold front that will inevitably end this Indian summer, I will watch as it comes, and watch too as the tree gives up its riches without a fight. From that release, from that surrender, I will learn and be reminded of the path that Meister Eckhart has laid out for me.

Forming Roots in Humility with Catherine of Siena

Winter is just around the corner. The wind howls with a vengeance through the cracks around our ill-fitting, aged windows, but I have discovered a way to fight the mood brought on by these gray November days: plant some indoor bulbs.

For the last couple of weeks, whenever I have felt my spirits begin to sink, I have reached into the refrigerator and pulled out another sack of the special bulbs I buy for forcing, growing in containers inside. The process of burying these small brown objects and watching them for weeks over the winter has a singular power for me. I plant what is apparently an inert and lifeless piece of matter, cover it carefully with soil, water it, and place the pot somewhere cool and dark while the roots form. At first, nothing seems to happen. I search for signs of life, but there are none, only flakes of dirt, minute pebbles, and the small glints of mica that make up the soil itself.

Then one day I see a swelling on the surface. The beginnings of growth are unmistakable. I bring the pot into the light where I can watch it. Soon green tips emerge, then leaves. A strong stem shoots up, capped with a bud. At last—when snow is still covering the ground outside, wind still whistling over the windowsill—the buds open, and there before me are yellow daffodils, lilies of the valley with their rows of tiny bells, pink tulips, or white narcissus that fill the house with their heady perfume. But that is far away. It is only November, and in these last few weeks of autumn, I must be patient and content with forming roots.

When I imagine the roots of a tree or a flower, I think of tough and supple cords, tubes that are strong enough to penetrate the soil, to travel far from the plant in search of nourishment. Tough and resilient, roots can navigate around rocks, dive to find deep water. Powerful, they can help the plant withstand the shifting of terrain or the onslaught of frost, foraging animals, or errant gardeners.

To be well rooted, then, suggests strength, power, tenacity, durability, a base to be reckoned with. So it is with some pause that I read this from Catherine of Siena, for whom the human soul is like a tree: "What gives life to both the tree and its branches is its root, so long as that root is planted in the soil of humility." What could it mean to be rooted in humility? It suggests grounding of a different kind: in deference, in reflection, in letting go, in a concept of self that is not assertive and does not seek its own glory. What is humility for Catherine, and why does everything depend on it?

Saint Catherine of Siena, a contemporary of Julian of Norwich, lived only thirty-three years, but her short life—unlike Julian's— was one of action and service. She was a preacher, a nurse, an advocate of the poor, a political activist, and an inveterate letter writer. She had the ear of the pope and was loved by the people of her region. Her active life, however, was grounded in years of solitude and contemplative prayer.

Catherine was born in 1347 in Siena, Italy. She was the daughter of a prosperous wool dyer. Her family lived in a brick house at the foot of a hill that was crowned by the church and cloister of San Dominico. The twenty-third child of twenty-four, Catherine seemed to know her destiny at a young age. She was a vivacious, attractive little girl. At the age of six, she began having visions of Christ. At the age of seven, she vowed to remain celibate forever. Her family, who doted on her, would have none of it. They made her do household labor and took away her privacy to distract her from her prayers. They threatened to marry her off.

Nothing would deflect Catherine from her path. She chopped off her lovely long hair and began spending more and more time at the cloister. At last, legend has it, when her father walked into her room one day while she was praying and saw a white dove over her head, he accepted her vocation and convinced the family to support her chosen path.

While she was still in her teens, Catherine joined a lay order of the Dominicans and donned the black-and-white habit of a *mantellata*. She spent the next three years in solitude and contemplative prayer, living at home and leaving only to go to Mass. The intensity of her visions increased. Catherine began thinking of Christ as her bridegroom, and her spiritual life focused on giving her heart and will entirely to him. This was a crucial moment in her life; Christ told her that she must give up her solitude and devote the rest of her days to service and love of her neighbor.

For the next thirteen years, Catherine dedicated herself to relieving the pain and desperation she saw around her, partly through direct service and partly through political action— speaking, preaching, and advocating through her letters. Bubonic plague was ravaging Siena, and corruption was degrading her beloved church. While Catherine was caring for the sick and dying Sienese people, she was also working desperately to bring about church reform and convince the pope to return to Rome from his temporary seat at Avignon.

In the last years of her life, Catherine wrote her major work, *The Dialogue*. Weakened by the effects of many years of little sleep and much fasting, during which she is said to have lived on the Communion wafer alone, Catherine dictated most of her book in an ecstatic state. Dense and repetitive, it takes the form of a dialog between Catherine and God, in which she makes four petitions: for herself, for reform of the church, for peace, and for the welfare of the whole world.

Catherine's approach in *The Dialogue* is one that I have found useful as well. I once attended a workshop in which I learned Ira Progoff's intensive journal system of process meditation. Essentially, it engages the participant in writing a series of dialogs: dialogs with parents, with friends or mentors, with works, with the body, with wisdom figures. Time and again I came to fascinating insights just from articulating on paper both sides of such an imaginary conversation. Catherine's dialog with God was an early precursor and, who knows, perhaps an inspiration for this modern, effective approach to personal growth.

❧

Catherine's biographer and confessor, Raymond of Capua, tells us in his biography of Catherine that the foundation of all her teaching lay in an early vision in which God taught her about humility: "Do you know, daughter, who you are, and who I am? If you know these two things, you will be blessed. You are she who is not; whereas I am He who is. Have this knowledge in your soul and the Enemy will never deceive you." Catherine was also told to learn to emulate Jesus in his suffering and begin "to see sweet things as bitter, bitter things as sweet."

Echoes of this vision appear in the first part of *The Dialogue*, in which God and Catherine talk about the soul being rooted in humility. True humility, God declares, is born of self-knowledge: "You will find humility in the knowledge of yourself when you see that even your own existence comes not from yourself but from me." This is insight born of years of self-examination in the contemplative life. When we look long enough and learn to see through all the illusions brought about by our selfish desires, we come to recognize our true self. As Carol Lee Flinders says in an essay on Saint Catherine, "When we manage to silence the voice that shouts 'I am,' then, in that silence, our deepest and truest self can speak. 'Not I, not I,' said the apostle Paul, 'but Christ liveth in me.'"

I used to think self-knowledge was simple. As I watched myself interact with people and perform certain tasks, I learned what distinguished me from others. I began to get a sense of myself, to watch a portrait emerge of this character on life's stage. I learned, for example, that I am cheerful, organized, friendly, and assertive. I learned that I am a leader who can get things done. Over the years, these qualities became identified in my mind with me, the person I was.

Gradually, however, I have begun to realize that these are only the shiny sides of the coins I have positioned to face outward, to represent my worth to the world. Though I am known as outgoing, I have a powerful introverted side. I am often cast in leadership roles, but I am learning to like the part of me that would far rather follow. I am cheerful, but I have discovered a long-untapped reservoir of tears. I have always been inclined to control, but I am learning that what works is letting go. Every quality becomes known to us in comparison with its opposite. "Light is seen better in contrast to darkness, and darkness in contrast to light," says God to Catherine. We cannot understand pain without pleasure, up without down, heavy without light. One cannot exist without the other; they are inextricably bound together, an inseparable whole.

To know myself, then, is to know my whole self. It is to seek out the qualities that have become submerged, that conditioning and reinforcement have forced underground. It is to understand that I cannot claim any one place on the spectrum for myself, but must embrace the totality of being that lies within me as my potential true self. For each aspect of myself, I only borrow from the whole. I dip into the rich ground of being that is common to us all.

To know myself is to see all that I have in common with others, to realize that they too contain in themselves the complete potential of human life in all of its complexity. It is also to recognize that insofar as we find others wanting, it is only knowledge of which we are deprived. Finally, to know myself is to see that I am only a conduit, a limited manifestation in time and space, a finite reflection of God, the one, the ground of all being.

When the youthful Catherine was spending her three years in solitude, she wrestled with demons—voices, the droning of insects, and bizarre sexual images that haunted and tortured her. Her biographers tell us that she finally conquered them when she remembered the words of her vision, to accept "the bitter as sweet." As soon as she embraced the suffering and stopped fighting the demons, they disappeared.

I have begun to learn, in my months of meditation practice, that the thoughts that buzz around in my head are only thoughts. Though they capture my attention and dominate the screen of my consciousness for the moment, they are not me. Catherine realized that the demons lived in her mind, but they were not part of her, that her true self lay deeper, beyond these passing illusions.

If humility is the opposite of pride, it is not that we must stop being proud of ourselves. Rather, we should understand a whole new meaning of "self." I am not merely a collection of my qualities, inclinations, or accomplishments, both good and bad. I am not my thoughts, my feelings, my fears, my aspirations. On close inspection, those are revealed to be only fleeting impressions. Pride comes from identifying with what can be measured, assets that I can acquire or improve. What I thought was my self is an illusion. The truth lies deeper, in looking beyond the boundaries of ego, beyond the limits of personality to the real source of my strength.

God says to Catherine, "This knowledge of yourself, and of me within yourself, is grounded in the soil of true humility. . . . This tree, so delightfully planted, bears many-fragranced blossoms."

ॐ

Catherine "saw that the soul passes through these stages with tears, so she wanted Truth to show her the difference among the kinds of tears, what was their source, and how they came to be, what fruit was to be had from such weeping." If a bulb is covered with dry soil, it will rest there in the same state, and nothing will happen. Only when it is watered, when the soil is made spongy and fragrant with moisture, will the bulb respond and begin to grow roots. Is it like this with my spirit? Are tears the water without which my soul will languish?

I read the newspapers now, and so often I weep over the stories. I never used to react like this. I cried for the last bear in the Sarajevo zoo, who died because there was no food for him. I cry over the skeletal bodies in Somalia, over stories of Minneapolis mothers who cannot buy Christmas presents for their families, over gun-toting children who cannot know peace in their lives.

The other morning, in my twenty minutes of meditation, I began saying as I often do the prayer of Saint Francis, repeating the verses slowly, one word at a time. I finished only the first line, "Lord, make me an instrument of thy peace," and suddenly from nowhere, from the depths of me, came tears that would not stop. Liturgy and hymns often make me cry. What are these tears? Where do they come from? Why now?

Catherine has laid out for us in her *Dialogue* God's explanation for the stages of tears. Where do I fall in this spectrum? Is there wisdom here that can help me make sense of my own weeping? Stage one tears for Catherine are tears of corruption and sin, tears of attachment, of jealousy, of ambition. Yes, I have always known those tears.

Stage two is fear—fear, Catherine says, of punishment for our sins. If sin is rooted in a worldly self, then is the giving up of self a kind of punishment? My tears also express a fear of the unknown. If I give myself over to this process, make myself an instrument, what will become of me? "Now her eyes begin to weep, and her tears well up from the fountain of her heart. But these tears are often sensual . . . because of the root of selfish love." This fear of loss is proud and selfish in the sense that it clings to self.

I am still gripped by the illusion that the familiar patterns of my life, the dependable ways I have to make myself content, and the material comforts and sources of security are the stuff of true happiness and fulfillment. I am afraid to let go, to give the impulses of compassion free rein, terrified that they will upset the applecart and throw my life into chaos. The very weeping itself is unstoppable and frightening. If I could just hold back on the water, maybe the growth will stop, and this whole new order will just wither up and disappear.

It is not all fear. Though there is an element of true compassion in the weeping over the newspaper stories, for example, there is also what Catherine calls "hunger for spiritual consolation." It feels good, it feels worthy, to cry for others. There is a relief in that release that is nothing but self-edification. There is self-pity as well: Why can't I just live my life simply, from day to day, like others? Why is this happening to me? Why do I have to suffer this pain, this confusion, this fog of uncertainty?

I can only read Catherine's words with wonder and realize how far away is her third, and final, stage, the day of perfect weeping, the day when I can "give love to other people, loving them without being loved by them, . . . without any concern for [my] own spiritual or material profit," the day of "perfect Truth."

I have put the pots of bulbs into cool, dark places. Some are tucked into corners of the refrigerator, some in the garage. They will stay there now for weeks, with no apparent change. I will continue to water them though. And watch. I know what is happening now, but I cannot see it. They are growing roots, roots upon which everything else depends.

Wintering: John of the Cross

It is cold, and I find it hard to get out of bed in the morning. By four o'clock in the afternoon, it is too dark to read without turning on the lights. If it weren't for Advent and the coming of Christmas, I would feel like crawling into a cave to hibernate like a bear. This Minnesota climate makes it nearly impossible for all but the hardiest of plants to survive the winter. The ground is frozen and covered with snow, light is low, and the air is frigid. Bulbs are nature's response to such hardship. They give the plant a protective covering, a sort of survival capsule, that allows it to withstand periods of deprivation without freezing, withering, or dying off. Deep under the earth, covered with soil and submerged in darkness, the bulbs, like the bears, process the energy that they have stored and ready themselves for the spring that will surely come.

Saint John of the Cross tells us that the human soul is like this as well. Though we may have all that it takes eventually to burst into glorious flower, episodes test our faith, our spiritual ability to survive what Saint John calls Dark Nights of the Soul. In this Advent season, as we approach the winter solstice, I am impatient for the return of the light. It has helped to read John of the Cross and to begin to understand the power and the importance of darkness.

John of the Cross and his mentor Teresa of Ávila were the two greatest Spanish mystics. Members of the Carmelite order of nuns and friars, they lived in central Spain in the mid-sixteenth century. John, born Juan de Yepes in 1542, came from Fontiveros, a little town in a rocky, barren region northwest of Madrid. His father was disowned by his family of wealthy silk merchants when he fell in love with John's mother, a poor weaver, and wanted to marry her. John's father died when John was three, and John's mother raised her children in an atmosphere of poverty, hunger, and desperation.

John was a gentle person from a very young age. His mother's attempts to put him to work in a trade were not successful. He was drawn instead to caring for the sick, so he worked in a local hospital. A nearby Jesuit school attracted his attention, and he soon discovered that he loved reading and writing. At age twenty-one, he entered the Carmelite monastery and continued his studies in philosophy and theology at the nearby University of Salamanca, known for its excellent teaching and stimulating intellectual climate.

This was a period of reform for Spanish monasteries, one in which the orders—which had become lax, disrupted by the confusion brought about by the Black Death—sought to reclaim their original founding rules and to return to a stricter life that included fasting, poverty, silence, and enclosure within the community. Teresa of Ávila was a leader in this reform movement, founding a new order of contemplative Carmelite nuns. John met her in 1567, eagerly absorbed her vision, and a year later joined the group of discalced friars she founded, so named because they originally went barefoot.

In his life as a friar, John soon discovered that he had an exceptional gift for spiritual direction, an ability to counsel others and to intuit and support their spiritual paths. A small man, just under five feet, he was gaunt and dark, with intense, burning eyes. An inspired listener and guide, John spent years in close communication with the residents of Teresa's monastery and his own. Though she was older than he and had been his mentor in the reform movement, John became Teresa's spiritual director. The years of intimate discussion with men and women contemplatives fed John's developing vocation as a writer, and brought a depth of understanding to his classic treatises on spirituality.

John's spirituality took the form of a lifelong love affair with God, and it was as an artist—a poet—that he gave primary expression to the feelings associated with that affair. Though he is most often associated with his prose work *Dark Night of the Soul,* John would perhaps rather have been remembered as the author of the poem "The Dark Night," on which the prose piece is a commentary. In 1577, as a result of a dispute between the reformed and unreformed Carmelites, John was blindfolded during the night and taken prisoner in Toledo. Until his escape nine months later, he was held captive, flogged, made to eat bread and water, and confined to a dark cell. In that period, he composed many of his poems, including the lyrical, romantic "Spiritual Canticle," a testimony to his ability to find divine inspiration in the most desolate of circumstances.

For John of the Cross, the spiritual life is a progression to union with God, the beloved. As in any love relationship, separation from the loved one is seen as privation, and *Dark Night of the Soul* details stages that the soul must pass through in its journey to the dazzling light of that final union. It is an intricate and systematic progression with categories and divisions: the passive night of the senses, followed by the passive night of the spirit. (*Dark Night of the Soul* is a companion piece to *Ascent of Mount Carmel,* which precedes it and focuses on the active, rather than the passive, stages of the spiritual "ascent.") Though John was only forty-nine when he died in 1591, he had the spiritual wisdom of a much older man. His work is perhaps of greatest value to those who have reached an advanced level of spiritual maturity, but even I—as one of what John calls his rank beginners—can find much of value in his words.

As I read the story of John's life and learned of his skill at spiritual direction, I wondered what it would have been like for me, a woman of the twentieth century, to come face to face with this intense little friar. I assumed, because of the hundreds of years that separated us, that he would have had trouble identifying with me, and that there would be little in his advice that would ring true. I was surprised, however, to find myself profiled early on in his complex scheme of things. His descriptions of some of my attitudes and spiritual inclinations were uncannily accurate, even though they were written in the sixteenth century. Whether from here I follow the path that he has laid out for me remains to be seen.

Saint John introduces his commentary on "The Dark Night" by noting that the Dark Nights of the soul are a mark of spiritual maturity. They are given by God to those who have progressed beyond the level of the "beginner." He dedicates his first seven chapters, however, to what he calls the vices of the beginner, traits that the first, or "sensory," night is designed to correct. Before I read John of the Cross, I imagined—with my recent longing for solitude, my growing introversion, my fears and tears—that I was perhaps experiencing one of his Dark Nights. Now I know that I am not.

> It should be known, then, that God nurtures and caresses the soul after it has been resolutely converted to His service, like a loving mother who warms her child with the heat of her bosom, nurses it with good milk and tender food, and carries and caresses it in her arms.

The person who is newly spiritually awakened, says John, receives this nourishment and thrives on it, delighting in spiritual exercises, long periods of prayer, the practice of liturgy and sacrament. Even penances, he says, give a certain amount of pleasure.

This sounds like me: rising faithfully at dawn to do *pranayama* and meditation; waiting impatiently for Sunday to come so I can go to church, hear the music and the poetry, taste of the Communion cup, and kneel, giving myself over to the language and expression of the heart. I might even say that the sore muscles I constantly suffer from the rigor of Iyengar yoga is a kind of penance, one that I willingly pay. All these pleasures are rooted in the senses: in sight, sound, taste, and feel, and John tells us that though they are a powerful introduction to the spiritual life, they pale in contrast to the kind of reward the mature seeker will eventually realize.

These self-indulgences are not on the face of it so reprehensible, says John, but they are danger signs of excesses to which the spiritual beginner is prone. As he laid out these imperfections, these "capital vices" as he terms them, I began to see myself in them as well, and it has helped me to develop a critical distance from some of my early impressions of the spiritual life.

Discretion and moderation are as desirable in the spiritual life as in any other. A natural outgrowth of the sensual pleasures to be found in religious practices, warns John, is what he calls spiritual gluttony. Could it be that I am vulnerable on this score? Going to church has never been a duty for me. When I was growing up, of course, my parents didn't go themselves. There is no Episcopal doctrine stating that one has to attend services, or, if there is, I have not been made aware of it. The reason I go to church every week is that I love it, and if I have to miss it for any reason, I feel deprived. It is the same with my morning practice. I look forward to that hour of the day and feel good as a result of it.

Feeling good is precisely the issue John has raised. The spiritual life, he says, is about transformation, about serving God and humanity, about doing God's will. Trying to feel good is an outgrowth of the materialism in which my generation was raised, or perhaps an antidote to its legacy of strict upbringing or to family patterns of abuse or addiction. If prayer and worship become mere avenues of pleasure seeking, then surely they constitute gluttony of a sort.

A certain pride, John says, comes with devoutness; holier-than-thou is what we call it today. It is a satisfaction with our own spiritual perspective, one that stakes out the territory of righteousness and regards those on the outside as misguided or, at best, deprived. My own resolutely secular upbringing and my long-held horror of such sanctimoniousness have made me slow to regard my non-spiritual friends with disapproval, but there is no question that I have taken a certain satisfaction in my own commitment to practice. That, says John, is pure vanity.

We beginners are other-directed too, John says, out to impress our spiritual mentors, to make ourselves look good to those further along the path than we are. That describes me as well. I am eager to please my clergy, my teachers, my friend the bishop. I work hard to read, to learn, perhaps for learning's own sake, but also to catch up fast so I won't look stupid. I strike a pose of openness (I have always been willing to talk about myself), but I rarely give voice to my real moments of doubt, my fears, my selfishness. I am not sure that I am in this for the long haul, but my mentors don't know that.

Beginners seek and love praise, we are told, and I am no exception. This is exactly backward, says John. The mature spiritual seeker focuses mainly on his or her inadequacies, failures, doubts, and frustrations: "the more they do [in the service of God], the less satisfaction they derive from it."

There comes a time, says John of the Cross, when, having developed a certain spiritual strength and the beginnings of detachment from the selfish life of creaturely attachments, beginners are ready to take the next step, the Dark Night of Sense: "It is at the time they are going about their spiritual exercises with delight and satisfaction, when in their opinion the sun of divine favor is shining most brightly on them, that God darkens all this light and closes the door." The realm of the senses is suddenly engulfed in this night, and nothing is left but dryness, bitterness, and indifference. This is the path of purgation, a necessary step if spiritual progress is to be made. It is a distaste not only for the things of God, he says, but for everything: a true darkness, in which the soul loses the capacity for delight and sensory satisfaction.

I had lunch with a friend the other day, and, though we were deep in conversation, the subtle and delicious taste of the buttery pastry triangle filled with vegetables was not lost on me. As I walked the dog this morning, I watched an old man approach on a bicycle. Hat pulled down to his eyes, steam adding a shelf of frost to his bright, thick white mustache, he wore, in the buttonhole of his down jacket, a bright yellow daffodil. Where did he get it? It made me smile, and he smiled back.

Saint John tells us that when God plunges a soul into the Dark Night of Sense, God "does not allow it to find sweetness or delight in anything." I am still far too susceptible to the joys of living—to good food, to music, to sunny days, to the pleasure of another's company—even to consider that I might be in such a phase. But what about my new longing for solitude, the days when some things that once gave me pleasure feel suddenly flat, when people and activities take such a toll on my spirit? What about the tears? Can it be that there are degrees of the Dark Night? It seems to me that it is possible to take smaller, less severe sojourns in the wilderness.

The Night of Sense is followed perhaps years later by a much more profound and severe Night of the Spirit, in which a sense of utter abandonment, pain, and suffering appear to eclipse any spiritual gains that have been made. These periods in the darkness, John tells us, have unimaginable rewards: the development of true humility, deepened understanding and insight, self-knowledge, compassion, and love of our neighbor. Most of all, though, they result in the kindling of a passion that is otherwise unsurpassed in the life of human beings: the mature desire for divine union, in which "the spirit feels itself here to be deeply and passionately in love" with God.

Saint John has given me the gift of anticipation. When I suddenly find myself thrown into an extreme version of one of his Dark Nights, when I can no longer take delight in anything, no longer pray, no longer even imagine that there is a God, I hope that I will be able to return to his words and find in them reason to be optimistic. I will "liberate [myself] from the impediment and fatigue of ideas and thoughts" and "be content simply with a loving and peaceful attentiveness to God." I hope that I will realize that what is happening is a sign of spiritual progress, and not cause for despair. I need to remind myself as well that the brief moments of darkness I experience now are small footholds on the path and not a sign to turn back.

O come thou Dayspring from on high,
And cheer us by thy drawing nigh:
Disperse the gloomy clouds of night
And death's dark shadow put to flight.
  ("O Come, O Come Emmanuel," traditional Advent hymn)

In the ritual reliving of the life of Christ that is the cycle of the Christian year, Advent represents a time of yearning for Christ's Second Coming, but also the epoch between Eve and Adam's Fall and the Incarnation. It is a period of darkness, of waiting and longing for the Redeemer. It coincides with the shortest, darkest days of the natural calendar, when the spirit waits for the turning of the seasons that will bring the light, a parallel to the *metanoia* brought on by the birth of Jesus.

In the Fall of Adam and Eve, Christians believe, the world lost its innocence. The realm of time and space became cut off from its divine origins; the vision and understanding of its people became clouded by separation from their source. To appreciate Christmas, we must enter deeply into the meaning of what precedes it—to reflect on the human tendency to sin, to be off the mark, to be dominated by the concerns of self and the limited world of material pleasures. The commercialism of our modern Christmas season with its excess spending and overindulgence is metaphorically reflective of this darkness that precedes the dawn.

Christ's coming is a shock that reverses the natural order, the ultimate paradox. He is God in human form, eternity in time, a ruler who is a lowly peasant, heaven on earth. So now, today, during Advent, we wait patiently in the shadows. We have learned from John of the Cross that we need darkness to help us discover the light, that there can be no day unless it follows night.

I stare eagerly at my pot of narcissus bulbs and see no sign of life. Nothing but black, undisturbed soil stares back at me. What is this, then, but darkness and night working their magic? What is this, then, but the gift of winter?

Exploring the Interior Castle with Teresa of Ávila

The sixth of January marks the beginning of the feast of the three Kings, or Epiphany, which celebrates the journey of the Magi to find the Christ Child. These Wise Men, people of authority in the world, were being called to a new order, to worship the King of Kings— the child of a carpenter lying in a lowly manger. Guided by the star in the East, they made a long and difficult journey and faced temptation and danger, until finally they penetrated the darkness to gaze upon the child, this source of eternal light. In many countries, Spain among them, Christians wait for Epiphany to give one another gifts, echoes of the offerings brought to Jesus by those three royal pilgrims.

We are all of royal lineage, Teresa of Ávila tells us. Regardless of our station in this life, we all contain within us a vast and sparkling palace that is the human soul. Let us consider, she says, the soul "to be like a castle made entirely out of a diamond or of very clear crystal, in which there are many rooms, just as in heaven there are many dwelling places." Our own pilgrimage, our own journey to discover God, is along the path of prayer, and Saint Teresa's book *The Interior Castle* offers us a rich and dazzling allegory depicting the stages of prayer and spiritual progress.

It is perhaps fitting, given her penchant for the princely metaphor, that Teresa was born into a well-to-do family. In 1536, at the age of twenty-one, she arrived at Ávila's Convent of the Incarnation to take her vows as a Carmelite nun with a more-than-adequate dowry. Her father, a tax gatherer, had come from a family of wealthy merchant *conversos,* Jews who had been forced by the Spanish Inquisition to renounce their faith and convert to Catholicism. Not surprisingly, he greeted his favorite daughter's vocation with something less than enthusiasm. He tried to stop her, but eventually acquiesced.

At first Teresa found that her new home suited her style. She was assigned generous quarters at the convent, where the size of a novice's dowry determined her accommodations. A gregarious young woman with a ready wit and a gift for conversation, Teresa was much sought after in the convent's parlor, which habitually opened its doors in the afternoon to receive anyone looking for advice or companionship: devout young women, widows, or even men-about-town.

Teresa attracted men and recognized early on that her flirtatious spirit and outgoing nature would present serious obstacles in her desire to develop a life of prayer.

> I had a serious fault that did me much harm; it was that when I began to know that certain persons liked me, and I found them attractive, I became so attached that my memory was bound strongly by the thought of them. . . . This was something so harmful it was leading my soul seriously astray.

Evidently Teresa's reputation was not compromised by these encounters, but it seems clear that she found the atmosphere in the parlor to be a hindrance to spiritual progress. These conditions at the Convent of the Incarnation largely motivated her later efforts at founding new monasteries and reforming older ones so that the nuns lived equally, regardless of background, and so that absolute poverty and the solitude necessary for prayer were cornerstones of their existence.

After two years at the Convent of the Incarnation, Teresa was driven from the parlor by an illness so serious that she had to leave the convent to seek the ministrations of a healer in a nearby town. She lapsed into a three-day coma and nearly died, but she rallied and was sent to her married sister's farm to convalesce. There she read a book that was to change her life. Francisco de Osuna's *Third Spiritual Alphabet* was an introduction to mental or contemplative prayer, a method known as interior recollection, in which prayer is internal, silent, and ultimately passive. She began to see prayer as intimacy, as friendship with God, and the energy that she had previously squandered on casual social encounters began to be concentrated instead on redirecting her soul toward union with a lover God. Like Catherine of Siena and, later, John of the Cross, images and themes from the Song of Songs informed Teresa's spiritual life. Her gifts for the contemplative path found new inspiration.

Years followed in which Teresa continued to struggle, her soul a battleground between the forces of men and creature comforts and the greater life of the Spirit revealed by her continued efforts at prayer: "On the one hand God was calling me; on the other hand I was following the world." Seven of Teresa's brothers were conquistadores, out to conquer the New World and bring home riches. Back in Spain, Teresa explored the inner reaches of her spirit and hoped to find buried there a treasure no less precious. At age forty, she experienced a sudden second conversion:

> One minute Teresa was walking past an image of the crucified Christ recently placed in a corridor of the Incarnation, and the next, they tell us, she was on her knees, sobbing, repenting of nearly twenty years' indifference, and begging God to strengthen her once and for all.

From that moment on, Teresa devoted herself completely to Carmelite reform for the benefit of her fellow sisters and of her own growing intimacy with God. Her movement for reform occurred at a time of great turmoil in the church.

The Protestant Reformation, which was changing the religious climate of Northern Europe, was beginning to threaten Spain. Internal struggles between Spanish Christians, Jews, and Moorish minorities had preoccupied and isolated Spain for hundreds of years. Once the Moors had been defeated and many of them, along with a large number of Jews, had been expelled, the Spanish Inquisition turned its obsessive and cruel attention to any Christian movements that appeared to threaten the domination of Roman Catholic orthodoxy. King Philip II reined in whatever freedom of the press remained, and ordered the destruction of subversive texts like those promoting contemplative prayer or advocating ecstatic contact with God. Teresa, particularly suspect for her *converso* origins, was watched closely, and she had to struggle mightily against conservative forces to found Saint Joseph's, her first reform house of eleven nuns, in Ávila in 1562. That same year she completed the first version of her autobiography, *The Book of Her Life*, written in large part to respond to her ultraorthodox critics.

Five years later, in 1567, Teresa met John of the Cross, whom she later called the father of her soul. They began a long collaboration and friendship that would lead to the founding of sixteen more reformed convents and four monasteries. Teresa wrote prolifically all her life, carrying on an enormous correspondence and completing four major books, including her master work, *The Interior Castle,* as well as many shorter pieces. She wrote freely and spontaneously in the vernacular, and, though she struggled with the demands that writing placed on her time, she was pleased with the results and attributed them to divine inspiration.

After years of working tirelessly despite very poor health, Teresa died in 1582 at the age of sixty-seven. She and Catherine of Siena are the only two women in Roman Catholic history to have been recognized for their scholarship as doctors of the church.

❧

A true bulb is a complex piece of architecture. Its paper-thin outer skin encases layer upon layer of fleshy scales containing food for the future plant. I have sliced a bulb in half and seen this structure for myself. Within the bulb, protected by its outer layers, sits a tiny embryo flower, perfectly formed, curled, and waiting to be thrust upward where it can bloom.

For Teresa of Ávila, the human soul is not unlike this natural treasure house. She envisions the soul as an interior castle with many successive rooms, or dwelling places, surrounding the innermost sanctum. This is the place where God, whom she frequently refers to as His Majesty, resides, and the place where secret exchanges between God and the soul take place.

Like the bulb, whose outer layers are loosely fitted and often caked with earth, the outer reaches of the soul are its links with the exterior world. Just as we normally see only the outside of a bulb, many people, says Teresa, live entirely in the outer layers of the soul, captivated by the things they see around them, by the material world of possessions, by things to do and places to go, by challenges, honors, and rewards. They are so attached to the outer world that they could care less about getting into the castle. The initial dwelling places of the soul, like the first layers of a bulb, are marked with the residue of earthly life. The people living there have not yet made a commitment to the journey inward, toward the inner sanctum and union with God.

So often the progress of spiritual awakening is measured in stages: Meister Eckhart's birth and breakthrough, Catherine of Siena's stairs, John of the Cross's successive Dark Nights of the Soul. These are typically linear progressions outward, upward, or forward toward some higher or future destination. Teresa's journey inward, however, resonates with my own experience and seems to anticipate our contemporary psychological notions of the layers of consciousness. As we burrow deeper toward the innermost reaches of the psyche, paradoxically our arrival at its center takes us beyond ourselves. We find at our core that we transcend individuality and experience unity-consciousness. The transpersonal psychology of Ken Wilbur in *No Boundary,* or of Francis Vaughan in *The Inward Arc,* takes us similarly on a path that moves inward from self-consciousness to superconsciousness to self-transcendence.

Reading about Saint Teresa's glittering diamond, her crystal palace of the soul, I began naturally to reflect on which of her seven dwelling places I currently call home. The entry point to this castle, says Teresa, is prayer and reflection, and I have been dedicated to their regular, daily practice for many months now. Like the man in the Christian Testament who, after sitting by the pool of Bethzatha for nearly forty years, was ordered to get up and walk (John 5:2–9), I believe that I have been called in from the outer courtyard of the castle and invited through the gates.

It is clear to me that upon entering, as Teresa predicted, "many reptiles" have entered with me. She says that these creatures prevent us "from seeing the beauty of the castle and from calming down," and indeed I am accompanied by a number of my old companions: skepticism, rationalism, preoccupation, and busyness. They all nip at my ankles from time to time and try to nudge me back toward the door we came in.

Once inside the castle, Teresa encourages us to wander from one room to another, not staying in any one place too long. The key to ridding ourselves, she says, of the "many reptiles" is humility, and humility is to be gained by lingering for a while in the room of self-knowledge. Humility and self-knowledge are the roots, the *sine qua non*, of spiritual progress, for Catherine of Siena as well.

I have, of late, been spending considerable time in this first room. For example, I am learning that I am not necessarily the extroverted social animal that I thought I was. In the last couple of years, I have begun to balk before setting off for a party, in touch with painful shyness and a lack of self-confidence I have never acknowledged before. I am beginning to understand my manipulative side as well. I am afraid, for instance, of being disappointed on my birthday or at Christmas, so I remind my husband in advance and give him plenty of hints as to what to give me. I want to decide how our house is decorated, but my husband has strong ideas as well. I set up the choices for him in advance, options that are all acceptable to me. This isn't compromise, but control. I use tears or anger in many situations to get my way. This recognition is, I hope, the beginning of self-knowledge, of opening my eyes to my whole self, the complete spectrum from light to shadow. With that, perhaps humility will follow.

"If a person is to enter the second dwelling places, it is important that he strive to give up unnecessary things and business affairs," says Teresa. If she or he doesn't begin doing this, it will be impossible for her or him to reach the main dwelling place. I have begun doing this, haven't I? I did leave a full-time career behind. I have slowed down. I have begun to welcome solitude, to be careful about the activities and companions that I seek out. By no means am I free from busyness or "unnecessary things," but Teresa acknowledges that "there are few dwelling places in this castle in which the devils do not wage battle."

So I feel confident that I have entered the castle, that I have even passed through the first dwelling places, and that I am invited to wander into the next rooms. But where am I today? Teresa's comments on the second and third dwelling places are instructive.

The second dwelling places represent for Teresa a transition zone between an existence that is bound to the world and the wholly spiritual life. Those of us in this transition, she says, are convinced that we want to continue the journey inward, but we are still attached, "occupied in our pastimes, business affairs, pleasures, . . . and still falling into sin and rising again." We have, she says, already begun to practice prayer, but we don't successfully avoid sin when opportunities for self-gratification present themselves. These rooms are the site of more effort than is required in the first. We are increasingly aware of ourselves, of how we want to be, of the humility we want to achieve, but it is a constant struggle.

In the second rooms, we are more and more aware of people who have gone before us and who have resided closer to the center. We are drawn to those who seem to be spiritually evolved and who can be mentors for us. We are captivated by books, by sermons, by any means of access to wisdom. Still, the level of our attachment to the world is an obstacle to our continued progress. Our heads are turned by praise or esteem. We cling to the affections of relatives and friends as if to a lifeline, and the health and survival of our own body is critical.

Much of this rings true, but I am uncomfortable with the implication that in order to lead a deeply spiritual life, I must deny and devalue the world. As long as I am alive, it seems to me, I am meant to enter fully into life on earth, to appreciate God's creation, and to use my talents to their fullest. As long as I have a body, is it not intended that I care for it and develop its skills? As long as I live with others, am I not meant to make the most of my relationships with them?

If I seem to be in Teresa's second dwelling places, how do I know I have not moved beyond them into the third? Those residing in the third level of rooms, Teresa tells us, have "won" the battles fought in the second. They "long not to offend His Majesty," she says, "even guarding themselves against venial sins; they are fond of doing penance . . . and spend their time well, practicing works of charity toward their neighbors."

The dwelling places beyond the second, rich with imagery and promise of reward but also with pain and struggle, can only serve now as a road map for my future travels. They are at once fascinating and daunting, and I doubt now whether I will ever be able to achieve the humility or even the desire necessary to enter them. To reach beyond the third dwelling places, we will "have had to live in the others a long while."

In these second and third rooms, our whole aim, Teresa tells us, is to "bring [our] will into conformity with God's will." This is the key. Doing our own will is what stands in our way. But how do we discern God's will? How do we reconcile it with the existence of evil or with our human notions of justice? What does it mean to do God's will?

The answer, I am slowly coming to understand, has to do with an attitude or a posture that is, like the walls of the crystal castle, transparent. I am not a force sufficient unto myself that can or should take control or resist the course of events. Doing God's will necessitates acceptance at the deepest level of what is given, of what is. It means that I need to see myself as the instrument of peace Francis of Assisi tells me I should be. The answer is expressed most eloquently in Lao-tzu's *Tao Te Ching*, in lines such as this: "If you don't realize the source, you stumble in confusion and sorrow." Acknowledging that I am not the source can lead to true humility, to true self-knowledge. It is the first step in doing God's will.

The first three dwelling places in the interior castle, the first three stages of prayer, represent a period of settling down. They are achievable, says Teresa, by our own efforts, by human desire and dedicated persistence aided by the ordinary grace of God. The fourth stage through the seventh and final stage, however, are essentially divine gifts. They consist of the supernatural stage—the mystical aspects of the spiritual life known as infused prayer, or the prayer of quiet. They are received from God. Why should we read on, it occurred to me to ask, if we cannot affect our own progress or the ultimate outcome? Teresa hints at an answer: "The important thing is not to think much but to love much; and so do that which best stirs you to love."

In much the same way that John of the Cross saw his own spiritual progress as mirroring the stages of a love affair, so did Teresa view the last three dwelling places as representing the stages of this all-consuming friendship with God. The fifth dwelling place is the locus of a courtship in which the soul experiences a kind of death in preparation for a new life in Christ. In the sixth level, betrothal takes place. The rooms at this level are places of torment, pain, and purification reminiscent of John's Dark Night of the Spirit. Progress to the seventh and final level, the place where "His Majesty" dwells alone, culminates in marriage: consummation of the relationship. Teresa remarks: "One can say no more—insofar as can be understood—than that the soul, I mean the spirit, is made one with God."

Teresa's final dwelling place is a place of peace and freedom in which one desires only to please God, to do the Divine Will. It is, therefore, a place of service, for once the self has been transcended, there is only the other to look to. "This is the reason for prayer, my daughters, the purpose of this spiritual marriage: the birth always of good works, good works." Ultimately, then, Teresa transcends the dualism that seems implied earlier. The end of the spiritual journey for her is to give oneself tirelessly to others, to love, and to service.

In the very center of the bulb lies the embryo flower, perfectly formed. Growth and transformation for the bulb involve a process of release, allowing the potential of that embryo to unfold. At the center of our soul, the place where God dwells, we discover that the perfect realization of a self is its own transcendence. To reach that place, to allow our own transformation to unfold, Teresa has helped us understand that the obstacles before us are walls of glass. Only by seeing past them, by letting in the light, do we grasp that the ultimate power to move us to our destination lies in letting go, in surrendering beyond the limitations of the human will.

For the Glory of God:
Martin Luther

My pots have come alive. The first round of narcissus bloomed early in January, and I have just cleaned out another large basket of them, gently laying the exhausted stems in the kitchen wastebasket and readying the basket's plastic liners for next year's crop. However, I still have much to look forward to. The pink hyacinths are pushing bravely up, halfway out of the soil, and today I removed the first pot of tulip bulbs from the refrigerator, their eager tips peeking out of the soil, each one looking like a shark's fin breaking the surface of the water or a distant sail just visible over the horizon.

I love the work of gardening. I forget myself entirely. It is work, to be sure, both summer and winter, but the time I put into the planting, potting, weeding, cultivating, and pruning yields nothing in the way of reward except the sheer pleasure of seeing and enjoying the results. Some people garden for praise—to get themselves on a garden tour or in a picture magazine. Others sell their flowers, and a few garden for others to make a living. In its most common form, though, flower gardening is done freely, with a full heart and without any expectation of return.

Martin Luther chose this kind of gardening to illustrate the attitude that he says Christians should have toward all of what we call good works:

> Now Adam was created righteous and upright and without sin by God so that he had no need of being justified and made up right through his tilling and keeping the garden; but, that he might not be idle, the Lord gave him a task to do. . . . This task would truly have been the freest of works, done only to please God and not to obtain righteousness.

In *The Freedom of a Christian,* Luther wrote that as believers, as baptized Christians, we have already received salvation. He urged the Christians of his day to heed the teachings of the Apostle Paul and return to the notion that "faith alone, without works, justifies, frees, and saves." Though as human creatures we are sinful, and our behavior naturally falls short, we are made entirely righteous in the eyes of God and are forgiven and justified by Christ's Crucifixion and Resurrection. It is not necessary to do anything to warrant this state of forgiveness. Good works, the acts of love we perform toward our neighbor, or personal disciplines of various kinds are only to be done for the glory of God. They "proceed from the good person," a person is not rendered good by their performance.

Martin Luther observed that something had gone wrong. Through the years, the Roman church had completely reversed this position. Many church practices in Luther's time implied that good works were done to earn salvation. They were not performed for their intrinsic value, but rather to produce check marks on a cosmic scorecard that would, if we were diligent enough, result in achieving righteousness in the sight of heaven.

Justification by faith, "true Christianity," said Luther, "is unknown throughout the world." As Christians, "we are altogether ignorant of our own name and do not know why we are Christians." He added, "We are taught by the doctrine of men to seek nothing but merits, rewards, and the things that are ours; of Christ we have made only a taskmaster."

When Luther first raised this issue and other complaints of church abuses in 1517, he objected specifically to the selling of indulgences: a practice of the Roman church in which guilt and punishment for sins could be avoided by buying their remission from representatives of the papal establishment. This commercialization of penance had become, in effect, a form of religious taxation. Moreover, the church had appropriated the function of justification and salvation, one that, according to the Scriptures and to Martin Luther, belonged only to God. This objection and similar grievances were immediately taken up by a populace disenchanted with Rome and its excesses, and Luther became a standard-bearer for the movement that resulted in the Protestant Reformation.

Martin Luther began his career staunchly loyal to Rome. Fleeing from an unhappy home and a childhood dominated by a father who beat him regularly, he joined the Augustinian brotherhood at age twenty-two, determined to follow the one path of which his parents would least approve. "The severe and harsh life I led with them," he wrote, "was the reason I afterward took refuge in the cloister and became a monk." Six years later, he made a pilgrimage to the Vatican.

Luther became a priest and a doctor of theology. He was appointed to a philosophy chair at Wittenberg, where he was a brilliant scholar and a popular lecturer. He was a forceful character, and his considerable genius resulted eventually in a literary legacy that included more than six hundred titles collected in one hundred volumes, over twenty-five hundred letters, the writing and composing of nearly forty hymns, and the translation of both the Hebrew Scriptures and the Christian Testament into German.

Inevitably Luther turned his discerning eye and articulate voice toward the obvious abuses and corruption that were alienating the populace from the Vatican. He could no longer tolerate what he considered to be Rome's basic misinterpretation of the Scriptures, so he began to write about his objections in the vernacular, circulating his beliefs in the form of tracts and treatises that earned him a wide following. In December 1520, having finally provoked Pope Leo X to denounce him as "'a wild boar which has invaded the Lord's vineyard,'" Luther organized a student protest and burned the papal document condemning his teachings. Within a month, the pope officially excommunicated Luther.

Luther set about reforming religious life in Germany. He suggested that priests, while useful for bringing the Scriptures and sacraments to the people, were essentially on a par with those they served. He carefully analyzed the sacraments, retaining only baptism, penance, and the Eucharist, which he considered the most essential. Luther asserted that the sacraments were not works through which one could please God, but rather signs of God's promise. He insisted that salvation came from an act of grace, a gift freely given to the believer, and that though humanity was inevitably inclined to sin, righteousness was a function of faith, not merit. Sin, for Luther, permanently pervaded the human condition. Sin was a measure of willfulness; a "person turned in on oneself." Even so, sin could be continually pardoned by God.

Luther opened the sources of spiritual growth to the people, translating the Scriptures and the liturgy into the vernacular, and writing sermons and composing hymns that thrust his themes into participatory worship. His writings reflect an appreciation of good food and drink, gratitude for family life, and support for self-expression in dance, drama, and all the arts.

Luther's movement for reformation eventually took on a patriotic and economic cast, as tradespeople and members of the German middle class thought better of sending their taxes to Rome. German nobility rushed to appropriate church property in their domains to keep its economic fruits for themselves. Despite its nationalistic appeal, the movement soon spread into the rest of Europe, resulting in the Reformation, which was to end the papal monopoly and change Christianity forever.

As I was growing up, the words *sin* and *salvation* were not in my family's lexicon. As an adult convert, making sense of them has been a challenge. I had never particularly thought of myself as a sinner, yet the liturgy I recite weekly insists that I am. It had never occurred to me to be concerned for my own salvation, or anyone else's, yet this is clearly the crux of the Gospel message. Saving sinners was the purpose of the Incarnation and the definitive result of the Crucifixion and Resurrection. However, as I have reflected on my upbringing and recast my family's legacy in a new vocabulary, I find that my parents' notions of good works and cosmic safety were not all that far from Martin Luther's.

I grew up feeling unconditionally loved and utterly forgiven. My parents, young marrieds in the early 1950s, considered themselves modern. They instinctively grasped the notion, one that has now become *de rigueur* in child development circles, that a positive self-concept is an important ingredient in grooming a child for achievement.

My best friend in grammar school, on the other hand, was Catholic. Every Friday she went to church and, closeted in a booth, told a priest what she had done during the week that was worthy of repentance. She often struggled mightily to come up with things to say, and occasionally she asked for my help. We would wrack our brains to come up with incidents that qualified: teasing our younger siblings, swearing. Even thoughts of an evil nature related to teachers or friends seemed to count. Somehow, despite our not infrequent joint responsibility for these nuggets of sin, I managed to escape taking on my requisite share of the guilt.

The whole notion of sin was foreign to me. I had a well-developed ethical sense. I knew right from wrong. Clearly, teasing my sister was wrong. I knew that when I confessed to having taken a dollar out of my mother's wallet, telling the truth was right and taking the dollar was wrong. It never occurred to me to ask how I knew, to search for the source of those ethical judgments. In any case, I had never been told that the rules of right and wrong derived from God, from the Bible, or from anything related to religion.

Unlike my Catholic friend, I did not live with a sense of shame. If I did something wrong, I recognized it, owned it, and redressed it by confessing, apologizing, or paying for it. I never seemed to internalize it or adopt guilt or a propensity for wrong-doing as part of my self-concept. Watching my friend struggle with her sense of sinfulness, her weekly ritual of confession and absolution, was as exotic and just as removed from my own life as the fairy tales I had read for years.

When I began attending Episcopal services a couple of years ago, the whole subject of sin re-entered my life. I had been eager to experience the liturgy, to begin to let the wisdom of the prayer book enter my consciousness and to embrace the tradition. But I had not expected to have to read aloud the liturgical Confession of Sin, to acknowledge and bewail my manifold sins and wickedness, to profess that I was not worthy to gather up the crumbs under the eucharistic table. I was repulsed. This simply is not true of me, I thought. I'm a good person, an ethical and responsible adult. Why should I have to admit to something I do not feel? At first, I simply stopped reciting when we got to those parts. Then, as the rhythm and poetry of the liturgy began to sink into my bones, I did recite the words, but I fought them with lingering discomfort.

I have found that practice does indeed shape belief. Since I have been reciting the Confession of Sin on a regular basis, I have begun to see myself in a different way. Nothing in my character has changed. I'm no better or worse than I used to be. I just see myself differently. As I have read Christian thinkers and reflected on my own life, I have begun to see the value in acknowledging and fully owning my dark side.

Sin, it seems to me now, is an attitude, an orientation, the product of limited vision. It is an attitude in which an individual is concerned primarily with his or her own ambitions, image, and reputation. It is an orientation, for example, that leads to pleasure seeking. As a human being living in sin, I love toys and covet material things. I buy expensive clothes that I don't need, and I lust after men who are not my husband. It is an attitude that leads to power seeking. I want to be famous, to be on the cover of a monthly magazine. I want to be invited to all the best parties and to be recognized for my achievements. I want to win awards and have an important-sounding title. I manipulate my husband or my colleagues to get my own way.

For me, sin is an orientation that makes me thoughtless. I put other people down to make myself look good, fight to be first in line at the department store counter, arrive late to an appointment or cancel one for my own convenience. Sin is an attitude that puts self and ego first, an attitude that is, as the Episcopal catechism states clearly, the seeking of our own will, not God's.

Saints Catherine and Teresa tell us that we need to begin with self-knowledge, and some aspects of what I now consider sin are not immediately apparent. Psychological theory, in particular that of C. G. Jung, was not available to Martin Luther, but it can help us understand sin. Jung tells me, for example, that my *persona*—the personality and self that I present to the world, the way that I would like to be—is different from my *shadow*—the part of me that I have submerged, the unconscious hiding place for the things that I fail to see or do not want to acknowledge.

For example, I know that I am occasionally quite generous. I help someone, or I make a contribution of time or money to a cause I believe in. But according to Jung, a strain of selfishness undoubtedly lives in my shadow and must be dealt with. If it is not claimed, acknowledged, or made conscious, the shadow will make itself known in a number of ways. One way is called projection. I have a store of selfishness, but I may be unaware of it. It can come out, though, by causing me to project it on someone else. I may find myself obsessively irritated by, and gossiping about, a "selfish" friend of mine who does not give money away. I may get angry with my husband if he does not help me or someone else who needs it. My shadow side may simply act itself out in my own life as well. I find that I occasionally have an irresistible urge to go shopping, to spend money on myself, to buy something I don't really need. This could be the greed that exists in my shadow coming out and driving me in ways that I do not understand.

There are positive ways to give vent to the shadow, say Jung and his interpreters. The important point is to acknowledge the forces within. Carefully paying attention to what motivates our actions helps, so does creative activity that gives vent to these forces. Another way, according to Jungian theory, is to acknowledge the shadow in a ritual fashion. Even if we are entirely unconscious of aspects of ourselves, the darkness can be paid out symbolically. Religious rituals like the Confession of Sin can do exactly that. I recall that the sacrament of penance was one of only three that Martin Luther retained.

Not long ago, when my husband and I were on vacation, we attended an Episcopal church in another city. As we came to the end of the service, I had a funny feeling that something was missing. After reflection, I realized that what had been left out was the Confession of Sin, the segment of the liturgy that had been making me so uncomfortable. However, as the day wore on, instead of being satisfied with the omission, I was surprised to find that what I actually felt was an imbalance. Dwelling totally in the light had seemed to leave unacknowledged the darkness that I was coming to understand is needed for wholeness, for truth.

Carnival, as in New Orleans' Mardi Gras, the Christian festival this month that ends the period before Lent, is often celebrated with customs that involve masks: the symbolic means by which we present our persona to the world and disguise the hidden or shadow aspects of ourselves. The next day, Ash Wednesday, marks the beginning of Lent, the penitential season in the Christian year when all the masks come off. As believers, we are asked to enter into our own darkness, to engage in a ritual acknowledgment of this human and sinful nature of ours. In preparation for Holy Week, for the reliving of Christ's death and Resurrection, we are asked to pause and reflect upon that within us which needs to die. We are reminded with a symbolic spot of ash on our forehead that we are dust, people of the earth created with a powerful will that seeks its own glory, a false and limited sense of self that rules us and limits our vision.

I still recoil at the thought of a self-concept that is rooted in shame or guilt. I have brought up my son to think of himself as a good person. But I am coming to see the value of self-examination and acknowledgment of the whole picture, pretty or not. I now welcome these opportunities to shed light on my dark side, to recognize and own the full spectrum of my humanity, and to remind myself that there is another orientation, another attitude that is available to me, one that—if adopted—can save me from myself.

What, then, of salvation? I grew up assuming that salvation had something to do with heaven, with the reward earned by a life of good behavior. However, reading Saint Paul and Martin Luther has convinced me that salvation is the gift of an alternative kind of truth, one that challenges our usual concept of self and introduces a new order. Salvation is a gift founded not on individual achievement, but on love; grounded not in individual power, but in surrender; rooted not in personal ambition, but in universal justice. Salvation, it seems to me, is transformation.

The Gospel message is essentially a wake-up call, one that offers an opportunity for an alternative orientation. The Good News is that by the exercise of faith, by receiving this gift of grace, by trusting in a different truth, I can lead a better life now, today. If I throw away the masks, let go of my old concept of self, if I become an instrument, surrender my will, I will operate according to a new set of rules, and the game will change altogether.

What of good works in this new regime? I would not perform them to earn salvation, for in this new order, that has already been given. I would simply live a new way, and good works would be the result. I would, above all, practice love. I would be oriented outward, concerned not for what I can get, but for what I can give. My self would be a conduit for God's will—not a driving force of its own—so ambition and the desire for personal aggrandizement would fall away. I would see others differently as well, and my neighbor would become an extension of me. Martin Luther says, "The works themselves do not justify him before God, but he does the works out of spontaneous love in obedience to God."

This notion of service is not entirely new to me. I was raised by parents who were committed to public service. They were politically engaged, liberal, and dedicated to humanitarian values. Our family dinner table—and we ate dinner together every night— was a forum where these ideas were discussed and passionately advocated.

My mother was a Hubert Humphrey fan long before his name was a household word. She was active with the Urban League, working for fair housing, and she bought me records with songs that taught me about white racism. My father spent hours volunteering for civic projects, and during the summer, I was expected to volunteer as well. Religious freedom, tolerance, and ecumenism were ingrained in me from early childhood, even without encouragement to profess belief myself.

Human motivations are complex, and I have no doubt that my parents had some selfish reasons for their actions, but the message I received was that these attitudes and values were meant to inform my life as well. We had much to give, and much needed doing. I never heard the slightest suggestion that I should strive to be worthy of heaven or that there would be some sort of eternal reward for doing or thinking these things. Though my parents threw out the bathwater, they kept the baby, and perhaps they had a point not unlike Luther's in rejecting what they felt the institutional church had become. If salvation bestows intrinsic righteousness and a propensity for good works, freely given, then I was prepared to receive it, from the beginning.

In the garden, it is easy to give freely. I forget myself and am able to focus only on helping each bulb or plant to reach its full potential. But how much more difficult it is in the rest of my work. Mothering, for example: I must learn to let go of my own aspirations for my son, forget about what other people think of him and, by extension, me, and cultivate him as I would one of my orchids. I need to be respectful, accepting that he has been given his own set of talents, skills, and inclinations. And I need to stay mindful only of nurturing possibility, the best that he—when treated with humble respect and love—can be.

At the Guthrie Theater, where I volunteer many hours of my time, I need to forget about me and my own visibility and reputation, and focus instead on the art of theater, helping to create an environment in which the director, actors, and artists are supported and allowed to do their best work.

In the last couple of years, I have begun a new enterprise, a book publishing business. In this new business, my partners and I need to keep our eye on the purpose of it all: to bring the work of deserving writers to the marketplace and to air issues for the consideration of readers. As a writer myself, I need to worry less about praise and criticism and give my energy to the subject at hand, to expressing my deepest self in as true a way as I can. This is right action. It means humbling myself to the process and not trying for results, for praise, for profit, for power.

Martin Luther reminds us that in the garden, before sin, God gave Adam and Eve a task that was to proceed from pure love. They had no need to be justified. They could work hard with a full heart, and the fruits of their labor—the planting, the tilling, and the harvesting—would only reflect glory on their Creator. So can we, says Luther, bring our life back to the garden. We need first to have faith, to trust that we are already safe. Then we can forget about preserving ourself, surrender our need to win or to seek our own pleasure and feed our ambition. We can live, he says, as Adam and Eve were meant to: simply for the glory of God.

Of Seeds and Quaker Silence

In Minnesota our patience begins to wear thin at this time of year. We have endured more than four months of cold now, and still snow obscures the ground. The blanket of white laid over the garden is shrinking around the edges and taking on a porous look, but the silence underneath it seems to be at its most profound. The garden appears to know that it will soon be stirring to life and thus gathers inward strength for the weeks of explosive growth that lie ahead. They say that the sap is running within the veins of the trees, but I cannot hear it. I am still indoors.

Most of my pots have finished blooming, so I am left to anticipate the Easter lily and page through my ever growing pile of seed catalogs. These glossy treasure troves have been arriving in the mail in groups of three or four a week. They take aim directly at people like me. Their colorful pictures feature perfect summer gardens in full bloom, baskets groaning with an abundant harvest of vegetables, and vases overflowing with brilliant cut flowers. I page through them by the hour, planning new combinations of color, working up the nerve to try some new perennial that is just slightly less hardy than is called for in this northern zone of ours. I grow most of my flowers from small plants that I buy in the nursery each spring, so placing orders for seeds is reserved mostly for vegetables. Inevitably I order many more than my small vegetable garden can accommodate. I am seduced by descriptions of exotic California varieties: tiny eggplants that can be held in the palm of the hand, sweet carrots no bigger than my baby finger, French green beans that are long and delicate and tender. I cannot resist the selections intended for salads: a Napa Valley mix of mild and piquant-tasting tender young greens, the peppery arugula, the red radicchio.

When the shipments arrive—even though it is not yet time to plant—I cannot resist opening them just to see what the seeds themselves look like. The beans, for example, are plump and hard, and their packets bulge with heft and promise. The lettuce seeds, though, are so tiny that their flat envelopes seem at first to be empty. I have to close them up again securely so that the tiny granules won't spill out and be lost. I never fail to wonder at the reality that each of these small tokens holds the potential for a full-grown plant and perhaps the harvest of many meals worth of vegetables.

The early Quakers used this moment of anticipation—this juxtaposition of seeds and of silence—to express the essence of their spirituality: "For, grace is a spiritual inward thing," wrote Isaac Penington in 1678, "an holy Seed, sown by God. . . . Know thy heart more and more ploughed up by the Lord, that his Seed's grace may grow up in thee more and more, and thou mayst daily feel thy heart as a garden." In a 1659 letter, George Fox wrote, "Your growth in the Seed is in the silence." Silence, for the Quakers, was the medium through which the Holy Spirit could be heard, through which they received divine guidance.

The Quakers never intended to be a sect. They were originally a small band of thoughtful and honest seekers who objected to the direction the Protestant movement had taken and set out only to reform the church of England. Echoing Martin Luther, they protested that paid preachers had too much of a platform and too much power. They objected that the Anglicans still clung to the notion of an infallible church and imposed too much uniformity on worship through the *Book of Common Prayer*. The Society of Friends began in the 1650s in Britain at a time when civil war had produced a climate of political and spiritual unrest. Democracy was the rallying cry on the political side, and many religious people insisted that everyone was equal in the sight of God.

George Fox, a shepherd and leather worker, had a series of mystical experiences that moved him to urge for more satisfying support and response from the religious establishment of the church of England. Finding no sympathy there, he organized a band of like-minded people called the Valiant Sixty, who went out two by two and agitated in churches, often being thrown out and occasionally beaten for their efforts. Frustrated in their attempts at reform, they began to meet together in groups for silent worship, and gradually the positive aspects of what they stood for began to emerge.

They became known as the Religious Society of Friends. Later, Fox wrote, it "was Justice Bennet of Derby that first called us Quakers because we bid them tremble at the word of God." Indeed, experience of God's word moved them to insist that revelation had not ceased with the Apostles, and that ordinary women and men could still be led by the Holy Spirit and the transforming power of Christ within.

The Friends were reminiscent of the early Christians in the time of the Apostle Paul. A determinedly lay movement, they met in small groups in kitchens in private homes, and in barns. Women and men shared power on an equal basis, and though the Friends resisted ritual, their own customs of participation marked them off from the religious establishment around them.

As the movement grew, it developed its unique brand of Christian worship. The group took its cue from the Gospels: "'For where two or three are gathered in my name, I am there among them'" (Matthew 18:20). With the Friends, the mystical dimension of Christianity took on a corporate character, based on collective silence and obedience. Private and family prayer were practiced, but the heart of classical Quakerism was the meeting.

The Friends' meetings were unprogrammed and involved no paid clergy. The members simply sat together in silence and waited for God to gather them inwardly so that the Holy Spirit could use individual members as a vehicle or mouthpiece. The Quakers preserved the contemplative tradition of prayer in their emphasis on silence. Discernment was important: to wait until it was clear whether one was being spoken to or called upon to speak or take action. They promulgated no formal creed. The fresh and immediate inner guidance they received was more important. The sense of the holiness of daily life and of every life relationship rendered such rituals as the sacraments redundant. George Fox knew the Bible almost by heart, and most Friends studied and prayed with the Bible in private and within the family. Scripture reading was not, however, a formal part of the service. An ecumenical attitude among the Friends respected and welcomed the wisdom of spiritual literature from other traditions.

The Quakers became known for more than their unique form of worship. They were remarkably honest people, distinguished by integrity and simplicity. Pacifists, the Friends adamantly opposed war or physical violence in any form. They wore plain clothing to emphasize the egalitarian nature of their movement, and they used the polite "thee" and "thou" form of address long after the custom had died in the popular usage. Tolerant and accepting, they reached out to American Indians in the early colonies and worked for the abolition of slavery. William Penn articulated the Friends' basic principles of human rights in the constitution he wrote in 1682 for the colony of Pennsylvania; much of its spirit was incorporated into the preamble and articles of the Constitution of the United States, written nearly one hundred years later.

Though the journal of George Fox is perhaps the best known of Quaker works, the rich spiritual tradition of this group is reflected in the many surviving letters and diaries of early Friends, such as those of Isaac Penington and John Woolman, and in the more recent writings of Caroline Stephen, Rufus Jones, Thomas R. Kelly, and Douglas V. Steere.

꙳

When entering an Episcopal church for worship, customarily a worshiper kneels briefly for a silent prayer before sitting in the pew to wait for the service to begin. For me, it is a moment that never fails to leave me frustrated. I come in full of distractions, and though I have entered sacred space, I am still tethered to the world outside by the racing of my mind, the busyness that continues to vibrate throughout my body. I kneel, but I am conscious of those around me, aware of my posture. I close my eyes, and nothing comes. I haltingly offer fragments of prayer, grasping for some phrase that will begin to still my mind, to bring me to the inward silence that the occasion deserves. But inevitably I sit before I am ready. It just won't work, I think to myself. I have been kneeling so long I am conspicuous, the service is about to begin. So it goes, week after week.

How refreshing it is to read about the Quaker meeting and the absolute reverence that is afforded this process of entering the silence. The group assembles, sits, and slowly allows itself to make a transition from the outside world. According to Douglas Steere in his introduction to *Quaker Spirituality*, it "takes some time for a meeting to be inwardly gathered." Each person in his or her own way, through simple gratitude, carefully learned techniques of centering to achieve the concentration necessary to be worthy of the task at hand—in Isaac Penington's words, to "be still and quiet, and silent before the Lord."

I understand the power of silence. It was only by being virtually forced into silence by my yoga classes beginning some seven years ago that I was able to start to acknowledge the possibility of a spiritual dimension in my life. I began a series of classes on Tuesday mornings in a storefront space not far from my house. The class was rigorous, and after an hour and a half of stretching muscles that had not been stretched for years, we were exhausted. We ended each class with a five- or ten-minute practice of *savasana,* the "corpse pose." We lay flat on our back on the wooden floor, all our limbs extended. The teacher then talked us through a process of complete relaxation, beginning with our forehead, face muscles, and neck, and ending with the tips of our toes.

Relaxing was hard at first, very hard. I would relax my arms, only to find that my shoulders had tightened up again. I would relax my knees, only to find that the tension had spread back into my hips, and so forth. Eventually I learned to make it through the sequence without the tension returning, but that was only the beginning. I learned that the hard part was still to come. Silencing the body was one thing, but quieting the mind was quite another. We were told to keep our attention on our breath, to watch it simply coming in and going out. Each time our mind wandered, we were to bring it back to the breath. What sounded simple was infinitely challenging. Distractions came and went; fantasies raged. Emotions surged through me, and returning to the breath was a near impossibility.

I didn't realize it at the time, but this process of coming to silence at the end of class was the beginning of what would be years of working to achieve concentration, stillness, and mindfulness in yoga postures, in meditation, in prayer, and in everyday life. Now I see that it will be a lifetime adventure.

This discipline of learning to be still opened for me the door to a whole new world. As I began to discern the difference between fleeting thoughts and emotions and the unchanging center point around which they came and went, I became conscious of an inner core, what the Quakers refer to as the Seed, that was my link with the Ground of all being, a sign of God's presence within me. I learned, as George Fox said, that silence was what allowed me access to that Seed, and it was in silence that its strength could be nurtured and encouraged to grow.

I rise at six each morning now, a time when it is dark much of the year in Minnesota. I leave my husband's and my room and go to one of the bedrooms that our children have left behind. There, with the kind of time the Friends know we need, I sit and enter the silence. It is a silence that is achieved with difficulty, and only on occasion. But when I do experience silence, it is—as Caroline Stephens writes—silence that is a "resolute fixing of the heart upon that which is unchangeable and eternal," silence that George Fox tells us will "mould [us] up into patience, into innocency, into soberness, into stillness, into stayedness, into quietness, up to God."

Angus has reminded me that he comes from Quaker stock. Though he was raised in the Episcopal church of his father, his mother's family were pacifists who left North Carolina during the Civil War. They came to Minnesota, and his grandfather started the first Friends' meeting house in the state. My reading in the Quaker tradition has explained a lot about my husband.

Though he is a corporate executive, Angus has never been particularly attached to the trappings of money or position. He loves the process of business, the challenge of keeping expenses low, the pursuit of an acquisition, and the intricate interactions of the people around him. Last year he was out in Colorado skiing with his son when the buckle on his ski boot broke. He took it in for repair, and when he asked the clerk how much he owed him for the work, the clerk replied: "Not a penny. Anyone who has the guts to wear a jacket that old around here gets work done on the house." It didn't take guts at all. Angus doesn't think about things like fashion or making a personal statement with the things he wears. Or is a jacket that old, like John Woolman's deliberate and conspicuous hat "of natural colour," a kind of statement in itself?

Angus has always had a streak of John Woolman in him. Woolman writes that "the Lord sent [him] forth into the world" and forbade him "to put off [his] hat to any, high or low. . . . Neither," he said, "might I bow or scrape my leg to any one." My husband is also not easily impressed. The very mention of British royalty prompts a lecture from him on their outrageous posturing. He has nothing but contempt for limousines and pretentious houses. Nor does he try to impress. He was approached at work several years ago by one of his friends who reminded him that any employee tends to "scale his car down from the executive officers'." My husband's modest car was causing his colleagues to complain that they couldn't buy the kind of car they wanted and could afford.

Most of all, though, my husband's Quaker streak comes out in the art of the deal. For Angus, a verbal agreement is as good as any contract. He lives by the principle of "being as much bound by one's word as one's bond." George Fox tells us that "people came to see Friends' honesty and truthfulness and 'yea' and 'nay' at a word in their dealing." Perhaps that is the secret of my husband's success. In any case, the respect he inspires from his business associates is a function of that elusive quality of honor that I can see now traces directly to his Quaker roots.

I have begun thinking myself about the applicability of Quaker principles to business. In our new publishing venture, the four principal owners have elected to operate in an unconventional fashion. Instead of choosing from among ourselves someone to be in charge, we have elected to go about our business as a quartet of equals, working together to make decisions when they are necessary and assigning tasks to the person most suited at the time to do what needs to be done. It is a relationship based on mutual respect and trust, and so far it has worked. In reading Douglas Steere's description of "Quaker unanimity," I found a perfect representation of the dynamics we hope to achieve, and I opened one of our meetings with a reading of it. Steere has coined the term *participative humility* to describe the kind of active but deferential posture one needs to have in group decision making. By participating, he says, I agree to put forth my best effort to contribute to the process, to make my opinion known in a reasoned, thoughtful fashion. I also agree to listen carefully and to be willing to temper my own position in response. When the sense of the meeting has finally emerged, I agree, even if it did not go my way, to abide by it and support it with a full heart. In summing up the kind of attitude aimed for, Steere quotes the French writer Alfred de Vigny, who once declared, "I am not always of my own opinion."

❧

When I was divorced and the single mother of a three-year-old son, I often had breakfast meetings that necessitated dropping my son off at his day-care center while it was still dark. I used to feel almost unbearably guilty dragging my sleepy toddler out of bed and into the cold, starlit morning. Inevitably though, when we arrived at his school, we would be greeted by Linda Sisson, a warm, ample, smiling woman who would welcome Phil with open arms and the cheerful announcement that there was cinnamon toast for breakfast.

I hadn't seen Linda for more than sixteen years. Recently, she was the one who, with the same warm smile, welcomed my husband and me as visitors to the Friends Meeting House in South Minneapolis. Angus had willingly accompanied me on my mission to experience the unprogrammed Quaker meeting that takes place each Sunday morning at 8:45.

The former Catholic church had had its stained-glass windows removed, its outside walls painted a natural brown, and its altar and pews replaced with simple chairs arranged in several concentric circles. We settled into two chairs and watched as about twenty-five people arrived singly and in pairs and scattered themselves evenly throughout the space. The oldest was a man who appeared to be in his late sixties, bearded, dressed all in brown with wide suspenders, and looking as if he had stepped right out of the pages of George Fox's journal. There were a few others in their fifties, but most were younger—baby boomers—with the natural, unpretentious look of veterans of the sixties who might be redirecting their anti–Vietnam war sentiments into environmental action. I felt at home among these people, imagining that some, like me, must surely be former Peace Corps volunteers.

I closed my eyes and began to ease myself into the silence. It was comfortable, and I found that I could readily assume the mental posture that I am used to in my morning sessions at home. Gradually I forgot my surroundings and began slowly, silently, to repeat the Saint Francis prayer as I often do. Soon the familiar rhythm of the words, falling one after another into the bottomless well in the center of my being, brought me to stillness and peace. After a long time, perhaps half an hour or so, a woman's voice broke the silence. She was experiencing some guilt, she said, and she needed only to say that out loud. She had received an image of hanging her guilt out in the light, like clothes on a line. She added that she was moved to wish that all the guilt of the world could, in the same way, be "brought into the light of forgiveness." It was a powerful image, and I could feel a collective acknowledgment of her gesture, a gentle shifting of energy in the room to focus on her need.

Many minutes later, a man spoke, as Isaac Penington often puts it, "in as few words as possible and as many as are necessary." His message was simple: "It is our God who speaks, who reaches to teach us in every thing." The beauty of his words echoed in my mind and began repeating like a new mantra as I sat in the silence. One other woman spoke up, reminding us of Robert Frost's words about home, and commenting that a "spiritual home" was a place to seek clarity, love, and forgiveness. After she spoke, it was clear that the profound silence was irretrievable. Perhaps spontaneously, perhaps at a signal, the Friends leaned toward one another, shaking hands solemnly and simply with their neighbors on every side.

Before the meeting closed, a convener invited us to introduce ourselves, one after another. Most seemed to be regulars. There were a couple of other guests. Most said only their name. A few took the opportunity to share personal concerns. At 9:45 it was over.

The people were warm, welcoming, and friendly to my husband and me. They were fascinated with the story Angus had, in introducing himself, told of his great-grandfather Lindley's founding of the Minnesota Quakers, and one history buff in the group confirmed that though the location had changed over the years, indeed this was the same meeting that Lindley had established in 1863.

It was refreshing, this service-without-ritual. In its meditative mode, it resembled my own daily practice, but the collective silence had a power that I cannot achieve on my own. I vowed to resume my efforts to find a group of people with whom to practice silent prayer on a regular basis. Still, it was not enough. The time-tested liturgy of the Episcopal service had an undeniable power for me. It provides a touchstone, a tuning fork that anchors me and brings me back to tradition, to the Scriptures, to the rhythm of the Christian year. It gives me structure, and, though I provide my own meaning, my own response, each time it offers me a rich well of imagery on which to draw.

⁂

March ends this year on Maundy Thursday. The service commemorates the Last Supper, the night before the Crucifixion. At this Passover meal, the last that Jesus was to share with his disciples, he instituted the Eucharist, the sacrament of bread and wine that was to become for many the center of Christian worship. Toward the end of the Saint Mark's service, the lights in the sanctuary are dimmed. Piece by piece, item by item, the altar is stripped of all its decoration. The velvet cushions, the books, the chalice, the flowers, the candles, and the silk embroidered cloths are ceremoniously removed. The cross, which remains, is covered with a black veil. The altar, now totally bare except for the shrouded cross, is plunged into darkness. The congregation sits quietly, meditatively, then files out in total silence into the night.

This stripping of the altar, this silence, is what George Fox and his Friends have prescribed for Christians everywhere. Seeing those things removed, those material goods of fine cloth and precious metal, reminds us of their transience and relative impotence. Even to drape the cross, to hide it, is a reminder that the symbols and rituals of religious practice, though rich and suggestive, are themselves only intermediaries, signposts along the way.

We are left, like the garden under its blanket of white, with silence. Gradually, with deliberate care, by focusing our mind and gathering ourself inward, we strip away the distractions of daily life, the attachments that keep bubbling up and hooking our attention, pulling us away from concentration and stillness. What is left is pure receptivity, pure transparency: a medium in which the Seed can grow and the Spirit can be heard.

Blooming:
Dorothy Day

April offers a whole new world.
The rains have pounded out the
last of the snow, and the earth
smells strong, like the spongy,
fertile carpet of a wet forest
floor. Birds fly overhead, trail-
ing long wisps of grass for the
nest building that is madly going on, and flowers are everywhere. The crocuses have
bloomed, poking their cheerful purple, white, and yellow
heads up from under the big
oak tree in the backyard, and the
stark white trunk of the birch is
ringed with bright blue scylla.

April began with Easter, the
liturgy calling us to new life and resurrection, and the
garden has picked up the theme with enthusiasm. Each plant that
spent so long underground, absorbing moisture and nourishment,
has now burst forth, ready to bestow its gift upon the world. A
flower is, after all, a social phenomenon: it is designed to be attractive to other creatures. Its color and perfume, nectar and pollen
attract the bees who fertilize it, helping it to procreate. Flowering
allows the plant to connect with the world around it, to fulfill its
purpose, before it withers and returns to the soil from which it
came. As a witness to this display, I am reminded that this is where
we too are headed.

The spiritual life—which is rooted in stillness, self-knowledge, prayer, and contemplation—is only truly realized in action, in reaching out to others, in opening to the world, in connection, and in community. It is for generative activity, for blooming, that we are born.

No one in the twentieth century better exemplifies the spiritual life in action than Dorothy Day. Founder of the Catholic Worker Movement and editor and publisher of its newspaper, she was an ardent advocate for poor and oppressed people of her time. More than an idealist, she went beyond lip service and opened hospitality houses that gave food and shelter to those whose causes she articulated. She marched for rights and for peace; she served time in jail; and she traveled far and wide to give support to others of her kind. She brought together theory and praxis in a life that was one continuous gift to the world.

The product of a southern father and a mother from upstate New York, Dorothy Day was born in 1897 in Brooklyn, and spent her childhood on the move. Her family, she wrote in her autobiography *The Long Loneliness,* lived in New York, San Francisco, and Chicago, following the twists and turns of her father's newspaper career. As she grew, Dorothy was a keen observer, and she saw all around her strikes, poverty, and injustice.

Dorothy was raised as a Christian and wrote later that she had always been "haunted by God," but she saw nothing in the way of vision or social change coming from the institutional church: "The ugliness of life in a world which professed itself to be Christian appalled me." At college in the Midwest, a professor whom she admired commented that people through the years had received much comfort from religion. She remarked, "From the way he spoke, . . . the class could infer that the strong did not need such props." Spurning such dependence, and disillusioned with the institutional church, Dorothy turned away from religion and sought inspiration elsewhere.

After college, Dorothy moved to Greenwich Village. She lived there, surrounded by poets, playwrights, artists, and idealists, and earned her living as a newspaper reporter. During a yearlong flu epidemic, she also worked in a hospital, but she returned soon afterward to journalism, her true vocation. She took an extended trip to Europe with a mysterious companion whom she chooses not to reveal in her autobiography. It was "a time of my own personal joy and heartbreak." Then Dorothy returned alone to Chicago, to odd jobs and a life of activism. She was arrested for her activities in the labor movement and went to jail, a degrading experience that radicalized her even further. She spent a brief stint in New Orleans, and then, at age twenty-four, she settled down at last in a little cottage on the beach in Staten Island, New York.

Dorothy lived on the beach with Forster—a British biologist and an anarchist, her soul mate and common-law husband. Her life there was idyllic: comfortable furniture with a place to write, a driftwood stove, plenty of books, and daily walks on the beach. On the surface, she had no reason for discontent. Her career so far had been satisfying, her experience broad. She had traveled and worked for causes she believed in. Nevertheless, Dorothy was plagued with dissatisfaction and felt that she was neglecting her talents and wasting her energy. A crisis came unexpectedly in the wake of her greatest joy: the birth of her daughter, Tamar. For years Dorothy had been drawn, in spite of her resolve, back to Christianity. She continued to be disappointed with the church, but she had an unquenchable thirst for a spiritual life. She had begun to read the Bible again and books like *The Imitation of Christ*. She came slowly to the realization that she wanted Tamar to be baptized.

Forster, on the other hand, vehemently opposed religion in any form. He raged against Dorothy's new habit of daily prayer, her weekly trips to Mass, her absorption in what he termed the supernatural. It became clear, she wrote, that "to become a Catholic meant for me to give up a mate with whom I was much in love. It got to the point where it was the simple question of whether I chose God or man." She held on, not wanting to choose a solitary life for herself and the child, but eventually she could wait no longer. She left Forster and sought instruction from a priest. Both she and Tamar were baptized in the Catholic church.

Back in New York City, she met Peter Maurin, a "ragged and rugged" Frenchman twenty years her senior, who became her mentor, collaborator, and fellow worker. This alert, animated, compelling man filled in the gaps in her knowledge of Catholic history and shared with Dorothy his vision for a new America. She wrote that Peter "aroused in you a sense of your own capacities for work, for accomplishment." Dorothy threw herself, heart and soul, into making their shared vision a reality. It was a brilliant, inspired collaboration. Together they sponsored roundtable discussions, opened houses to shelter and feed poor and dispossessed people, advocated for agronomic universities, and finally tackled the linchpin in their crusade for "bread and truth"—a newspaper.

They founded the *Catholic Worker,* a bold, uncompromising paper for the men and women on the street, and discovered a hunger among American Catholics for exactly the sort of anti-establishment advocacy the paper contained. This cheaply printed paper sold for a penny a copy and became a voice for the worker, the prisoner, the addict, the unemployed. It was consistently anti-war, at times against overwhelming opposition. Dorothy's pacifism was not negotiable. As editor and publisher, she authored the column "On Pilgrimage" for thirty years, to the month she died in 1980.

Dorothy traveled extensively, organizing and reaching out to people and causes that touched her. She went to Cuba, to Rome, to the fields of migrant workers, to Indian reservations, to urban slums. But this was not *noblesse oblige:* she wore simple hand-me-down clothes, lived and ate with the people she served, and stood beside them in their need. Undergirding all the protests, the marches, the advocacy, the beds, and the meals was a pervasive, unshakable compassion that informed everything she did.

If I am honest with myself, I must admit that I was not looking forward to reading Dorothy Day. I had heard about *The Long Loneliness,* about her inspiring career, but I knew that reading her work would force me to examine my own life and values, and that nothing but discomfort could come from such scrutiny.

I was born into privilege, the child of a comfortably middle-class family. My father, who had grown up without money, worked hard for a locally based milling company and did very well. By the time I was in junior high, my parents could afford to send me to a private school, and it was rare that I was deprived of anything I wanted for lack of money. By the time I was in college, my father was a successful investment fund manager. In his seventies now, he is still working hard. My parents live well. They have provided generously for their children and grandchildren, and they give liberally to their favorite causes.

Though I struggled as a single working mother for several years after my divorce, my own career developed steadily and, until I gave up full-time work eight years ago, I earned more than enough to make a comfortable life for myself and my son.

Now I am married to an executive of a Fortune 500 company. Angus too has worked hard all his life and been rewarded for it. For us, the problems of money are those of attitude: How do we keep from spoiling our children? How do we reconcile our own comfort with the struggles we see around us? How do we invest and contribute wisely, for the greatest good? How can we have money and be Christians too?

For Dorothy Day, voluntary poverty was the first requirement of the Christian life. She gave everything she had, consistently, without attachment, following Christ's admonition to the rich young man. From her priest Father Roy, Peter Maurin, and others, Dorothy learned that one reaps a hundred times what one sows, that to give away whatever meager resources she had would result in rewards both physical and spiritual many times their value.

However, is it necessary to give up everything to be a Christian, to be a good person? I spent a summer with Crossroads Africa and another two years in Africa in the Peace Corps. I existed in those days with minimal resources, living simply, but no less happily, no more virtuously than I do now. When I was first divorced and counting every penny as a single mother, I felt no more worthy, no better about myself ethically than I do now. In our current situation, I derive enormous satisfaction from being able to give generously to causes I believe in, to surprise a solicitor with a response that is more than was asked for, to solve a problem for someone with a spontaneous, unexpected gift. But is that only because it doesn't hurt? Is it really giving if it doesn't result in my own deprivation, my own suffering?

I have often rationalized that it is our attitude about money that matters. If we carry it lightly, give it away with ease, and regard its continued accumulation with indifference, then is its presence such a sin? I like to think I have achieved healthy detachment, but I am afraid I fall short. Am I not hopelessly materialistic? I still care about the way I look, and I spend too much money on clothes. I still trade in my car before I need to, still take pleasure in attractive living spaces, in a well-set table, in sports equipment that is up-to-date. How much more good could that same money do in the world if it were put to work in employment programs, in medical relief, or in a soup kitchen? It could do much, but on the other hand, the consumer spending we do helps to fuel our economy and provide jobs that might not otherwise be there.

My husband and I are politically liberal. We favor a progressive tax system, give generously to candidates, and pay our taxes willingly. We both use our personal time and influence to raise money for a variety of organizations and causes. Could we do these things as effectively if we were to divest ourselves tomorrow of all our worldly goods? Would the community be proportionately better off?

Still, Christ's words to the rich man are unambiguous: "'Sell all that you own and distribute the money to the poor, and you will have treasure in heaven; then come, follow me'" (Luke 18:22). Can I call myself a Christian if I ignore Jesus' words? Dorothy Day's answer, modeled in her life of voluntary poverty, would be clear.

If money was a critical issue for Dorothy Day, the use of time and energy was an even bigger one: "To pledge yourself to voluntary poverty for life so that you can share with your brothers is not enough. One must live with them, share with them their suffering too. Give up one's privacy, and mental and spiritual comforts as well as physical."

Mystics and contemplative souls throughout history all seem to agree that the spiritual life leads ultimately to action. The inevitable result of a life of prayer, of choosing a path that leads to God, is to learn to experience the presence of God in every being that lives. Meister Eckhart tells me that after the breakthrough, I will come to experience a feeling of unity with all things and an expanded sense of self. I will understand that the divine presence within me exists within every being, and when I encounter the other, I will be meeting an extension of myself. If I understand that, I become transparent, acting not to gratify my own ego but to serve a larger purpose, to become an instrument of right action, to participate in and contribute to a truth that is larger than myself.

Dorothy Day offered up any personal claim to worldly goods. She gave up her life partner, her lover. She sacrificed comfort and privacy, all for the principles of peace, justice, and the redistribution of wealth. The question for me after reading her inspiring story is, What constitutes right action? Is Dorothy Day's example one to be followed to the letter, or does it teach us lessons of attitude that can be applied to a wider range of choices for action in the world?

It is tempting at first to read her story as a literal call to action, Dorothy Day style. It is hard not to feel that one ought to embrace her politics and adopt her solutions. She was articulate and compelling in her descriptions of poverty and injustice. And even though we live decades later, the conditions that moved Dorothy Day in the 1930s and 1940s still exist. Workers are exploited; violence is a way of life; people are unemployed, hungry, dispossessed, homeless. How can I possibly justify not sharing my space with a family in need? How can I work anywhere but in a soup kitchen, a hospice, a shelter?

The cold truth, however, is that I am just not drawn to that kind of work. Dorothy Day was. Dorothy Day wanted to do it. She was driven; she had no choice. Though she did say that she "had a sense of guilt, of responsibility," it was not just guilt that drove her. An irresistible calling, a sense of purpose, overwhelmed all her other desires and drew her into poverty, into radical politics, and into direct relief activities. This sense of a vocation, or call, is most often associated with the choice to enter the priesthood or a monastery, but I am beginning to see that each of us, if we listen hard enough, can discern a similar summons. "There are varieties of gifts, but the same Spirit," said the Apostle Paul. "There are varieties of activities, but it is the same God who activates all of them in everyone" (1 Corinthians 12:4,6).

Aren't there as many legitimate and necessary vocations as there are worthwhile human endeavors? Someone needs to farm, to build buildings, to manufacture machines and useful goods. Someone needs to tend to the sick, to teach, to preach. Someone needs to design, to compose, to paint. If no one responded to these vocations, human life as we know it could not exist. As I grow and continually seek to know my own true vocation, what can I learn from Dorothy Day's experience that will help me both to discover it and to carry it out?

First, Dorothy looked outward in service to others—to the community and the world at large—to determine how to spend her energy. She did not focus on her own personal gratification. She did not consider the money or the status her work would bring. She did not think about the hours required, the location of the office, or who her boss would be. She saw what needed to be done, and she responded out of love.

Second, Dorothy operated effectively on more than one level. She aimed for social change, but she was also dedicated to work that affected one person at a time. Through her newspaper, she influenced public opinion and prepared the way for social and political transformation.

In my life, writing can do that, so can public speaking, lobbying, fund-raising, and publishing. Dorothy Day also took in individual families off the street, fed hungry men and women, and found people jobs. I can influence individuals through supporting members of my family or listening to a friend. I can lend money or give to someone in need. Most of all, in my day-to-day activities, in meetings or social encounters, I can act in such a way that I have the general interest at heart and transcend the needs of my own ego. I can use power for others' benefit, letting go of the need for control. In short, like Dorothy Day, I can act out of love and affect people, one at a time.

Third, Dorothy Day modeled an appropriate approach to action. In working with the poor, she was not voyeuristic or paternalistic. She did not make token gestures to assuage her conscience. She committed herself to her work. She lived and ate with the people she assisted. When the heat was turned off, she too was cold. When food was scarce, she also went hungry. From this I understand that I must not raise money for a cause unless I have first given generously, not agree to chair some effort without putting in hours of work myself. It helps to be a writer myself when it comes time to turn down someone's manuscript for publication, and, like my partners, I must put in time and energy to make our venture a success.

Finally, Dorothy Day had patience. Confronted with overwhelming needs, she responded as she could, when the time was right. So often I feel confused in the face of so many choices, so many demands on my time. My reading tells me that a call to action is the fruit of the spiritual life. I have only just begun to experience radical changes in my concept of self, of purpose, of will. I think that eventually these will lead naturally into action,

action that is right for me and that grows organically out of my individual skills and inclinations. I do not have to rush into decisions before I am really ready. These changes of heart take time; transformation does not happen overnight. On the other hand, when does patience become only an excuse for procrastination?

I look at my garden now after the long winter, and I see a riot of color. So much of the beauty and interest it offers is a function of the variety of flowers: some short, some tall, blossoms in every color and shape. So it is with our own blooming. As individuals, we complement one another with our talents and inclinations. As we come into our own and open ourselves to the world, as we listen for the call to right action, we can be of service in a multitude of ways, each in our own style. Dorothy Day represented a rare species indeed, but I may bloom in an entirely different way, and perhaps the garden will be the better for it.

Thomas Merton and the Walls of Freedom

A garden is not something found in nature. I walk around the yard now, in the thick of spring, and I admire the clumps of pink and white tulips that form a backdrop for clusters of sky blue hyacinths. A graceful bleeding heart arches over them, and yellow daffodils nestle under the lilac bushes. These are not accidents, these plantings that together make such a lively tapestry of color. The flowers would not bloom like this without careful planning, weeding, and cultivation. I have just finished planting my bean and lettuce seeds, and as I clicked closed the gate to the wire fence that surrounds their small plot, I was reminded that their bounty will be a function of this enclosure that confines them and separates them from marauding rabbits and hungry chipmunks. Order, discipline, and boundaries give the plants the freedom they need to thrive.

"So Brother Matthew locked the gate behind me, and I was enclosed in the four walls of my new freedom." Thus begins a segment of Thomas Merton's *Seven Storey Mountain,* and thus began his new life at the Trappist Abbey of Gethsemani, Kentucky. How is it that one might choose to enter a monastery—the paradigm of discipline, circumscribed routine, and commitment—to find freedom? In this early autobiography, written when he was only thirty-one, Merton tells of his transformation from a rowdy college youth of secular predisposition into a Trappist monk. He began wrestling in that book with an issue that would concern him all his life: freedom and its relationship to discipline, commitment, and obedience.

I have read *The Seven Storey Mountain* three times now. Over the last couple of years, I have gone on to read others of his works, each time getting drawn powerfully into them, caught up in the web of his words, unable to break the spell that they seem to cast over me. Why? What does a modern woman, a wife, a mother, a feminist, and a busy proponent of the active life find of interest in the reflections of a Trappist monk? Why does his strange language with its unorthodox capitalizations, its insertions of untranslated Latin, its dreamy, otherworldly quality appeal to me so?

I am not the only one, it seems. In its original 1948 cloth version, *Seven Storey Mountain* sold over six hundred thousand copies. It has been translated into at least sixteen languages and has sold millions of copies in paperback. Merton's voice clearly speaks to human longing. His decision to live in a monastery led him on a road not traveled by many who have a streak of the monk in them, a buried self that understands the lure of silence, of austerity, of solitude.

When Merton entered the Abbey of Gethsemani in December 1941, he was sure of his vocation, but the road there had not been a straight and narrow one. He was born in France, in a small town near the Spanish border, but he spent most of his early years in Long Island, New York, in the home of his maternal grandparents. His mother, a Quaker and a pacifist, died when Tom was six, and his father led an itinerant life as a struggling painter, reclaiming Tom at age twelve and taking him back to France. They moved again the next year to England, where they lived with an aunt and uncle, and Tom was put in a boarding school. His father developed a malignant brain tumor and died within a year and a half. At age fifteen, Thomas Merton was an orphan. He stayed in England to finish secondary school and then entered Cambridge University.

In his youth, Merton was, at times, attracted to the spiritual life. A couple in southern France, friends of his father, had been concerned about Tom's neglected religious training. They were staunch Catholics, and, though Tom retained an aversion to Catholicism, he admired them greatly and later credited them with awakening his soul. His dying father's last communication with Tom, after he had lost the ability to speak, was a series of drawings of Byzantine icons. Merton traveled in his late teens to Italy: "I was fascinated by these Byzantine mozaics. I began to haunt the churches where they were to be found."

These flashes of religious feeling were short-lived, however. Merton returned to college at Cambridge, and the next period of his life was filled with what he could only later refer to as "an incoherent riot of undirected passion."

> It was in that year, [1933,] that the hard crust of my dry soul finally squeezed out all the last traces of religion that had ever been in it. There was no room for any God in that empty temple full of dust and rubble which I was now so jealously to guard against all intruders, in order to devote it to the worship of my own stupid will.

College meant liquor and women. One night, after he and his friends had been drinking, Merton is said to have participated in a mock crucifixion. He bore a mark for years that suggested that he, in fact, was impaled through the palm of his right hand. He fathered a child out of wedlock with a woman who has not been identified. Though both mother and child were believed to have been killed in World War II bombings, a will Merton wrote at age twenty-nine directed a family friend to give half of his estate to the mother, "if that person can be contacted."

Merton returned to the United States for the summer and decided to stay, finishing college and entering graduate school at Columbia. He threw himself into student life, working on the newspaper, playing the piano, and reveling in song and drink. During his years at Columbia, almost in spite of himself, Merton found himself drawn inexorably toward a spiritual life and specifically toward the Catholic church.

Books—and Merton's friends and mentors—played an important role in bringing about his eventual conversion. Merton, like me, was a reader. He would pick up a clue in conversation and follow it up, and often clues such as this led him to books that were essential to his evolution. Dante eventually gave him the title for his autobiography, after he read about the "seven storey" ascent to heaven in the *Purgatorio*. He was inspired by the mystical poetry of William Blake and went on to do his master's thesis on him. Reading Blake convinced Merton that "the only way to live was to live in a world that was charged with the presence and reality of God."

Etienne Gilson's *The Spirit of Medieval Philosophy* introduced Merton to a God that was Infinite Being and gave him permission in the tradition of Meister Eckhart to let go of trying to define God and accept a being who "transcends all our conceptions." Jacques Maritain's *Art and Scholasticism* taught him about virtue and led him to see it as strength. Through the pages of Aldous Huxley's *Ends and Means,* Merton began to be intrigued by asceticism and detachment as a way to open himself to the experience of God. The book recounted Huxley's own conversion from a confirmed agnostic to a practicing mystic, albeit an eclectic one, who was influenced by both Christian and Eastern thought.

Friends and mentors have been important to my own conversion process, and Thomas Merton needed them as well to take him from Manhattan to the Abbey of Gethsemani. For example, Robert Lax, a college companion and confidant of Merton's, was tall, dark, morose, Jewish, and a born contemplative. He was a man of "natural, instinctive spirituality, a kind of inborn direction to the living God." Lax talked of becoming a Catholic even before Merton did, he recommended books to Merton, and he convinced Merton of the legitimacy of the supernatural order. It was Lax who urged Merton to join a monastery and become a priest, to aim high and not be satisfied only with joining the church. Lax did not himself convert until years after Merton entered the Abbey.

Mark Van Doren, Merton's professor in an eighteenth-century English literature class at Columbia, had a "gift of communicating to [his students] something of his own vital interest in things." He drew out the best in his students, extracting wisdom and explicit ideas they didn't know they had. Merton later became an inspired teacher himself.

Dan Walsh, a part-time lecturer at Columbia, spoke enthusiastically about the Trappists (Order of Cistercians of the Strict Observance), thereby planting the seeds that led to Merton's final vocation. The Hindu monk Bramachari, a visitor to New York from

India and a member of Merton's group of friends, deflected Merton with gentleness and humor from his fascination with the mysticism of the East, directed him into key readings in the Christian tradition, and modeled for him the value of spiritual practice. Father Moore of Merton's neighborhood church in New York "planted" the Catechism "in [his] soul" and prepared him for baptism. Finally, after Merton had been refused by the Franciscan order when they learned the details of his former life of sin, it was Friar Father Philotheus, a colleague at the College of Saint Bonaventure, who restored Merton's confidence in his vocation and encouraged him to pursue application to the Abbey of Gethsemani.

Practice was perhaps the most important element in Merton's conversion, but not until he moved out of his grandparents' house in Douglaston and took a rented room near Columbia did he find the solitude he needed. "Whatever else may have happened in that room, it was also there that I started to pray again more or less regularly, . . . and it was from there that I was eventually to be driven out by an almost physical push, to go and look for a priest." Merton began to go to Mass, to seek instruction. Only as a result of that direct experience did he reach a decision to be baptized. Later, he purchased almost on impulse a set of breviaries, four books that contain the canonical office, or liturgy of the hours of monastic life. By reciting the liturgy's ancient prayers and psalms and pondering its readings regularly, by absorbing them into his daily life, Merton came to accept his true vocation to the Abbey of Gethsemani.

❧

Deciding to enter a monastery seems, on the face of it, like choosing to enter a prison. The walls are thick, the life austere, and for a Trappist monk like Merton, there were the vows of celibacy and silence. Merton's decision would seem to deprive him of his freedom. But Thomas Merton wrote of the day he entered the abbey: "I was free. I had recovered my liberty. I belonged to God, not to myself: and to belong to Him is to be free, free of all the anxieties and worries and sorrows that belong to this earth, and the love of the things that are in it."

My stepchildren, who are young adults out of college but not yet settled into families or careers, grapple constantly with this notion of freedom. They resist marriage because it will mean giving up their freedom. They choose part-time jobs because they want to be free to do the things they want to do. A full-time career would limit their options, cut off their freedom.

What does freedom mean? Does it mean that we must leave open all the choices, face a dizzying and infinite array of possibilities? Does it mean that to be really free, to belong to God, we must give up all the options and renounce the world? I am wrestling with this issue myself.

With the help of the garden, I am coming to see that aspects of the monastery might have something to teach us about our life in this world. Without necessarily joining a monastery, we can think about freedom in a new way, one in which the number of choices open to us becomes less important.

For Thomas Merton, enslavement was selfishness, egoism, ambition, and a need for power. The lure of money and material things was a form of tyranny that encouraged people to manipulate and dominate one another. To be in the world, to live driven by these compulsions, was to be in the prison of one's own selfhood.

The path out of this trap was, for Merton, by way of the desert, a life of solitude. The life of contemplation—in Merton's case, life in a monastery—allowed him to see that these attachments cause us to construct a false self. To find out who we really are, we need to strip away the temptations of the world, turn inward, and find buried there our true identity, our connection at the core to God. As Merton says, "Freedom means, therefore, the complete destruction in me of all selfishness." By becoming transparent, by surrendering our own will and living in complete obedience to God, we find real freedom. A self planted in the world is like a seed sown in the wild: it seeks the light, tries to take root, but it can be overcome by weeds, choked to death by competition.

Do we have to leave the world in order to find our true self? I hope not. But even if we do not achieve the total freedom Merton envisioned, perhaps there are ways for us to make a start. Discipline and commitment, it seems to me, can offer those of us in the world some of the advantages of a monastery to help us quiet the voices, stem the desires, begin to find peace, and discover our true self.

The vow of celibacy, for example, allows a monk to concentrate all his energy on his relationship with God, one that eventually overpowers the desires of the flesh and keeps his drive for intimacy focused in the spirit. Marriage, for us, involves a similar vow. By committing to a life with Angus, I provide myself with an outlet for physical desire that helps free me from the need to be driven by it in my relationships with others. By concentrating my energies on one long-term relationship, I am freed from the need to work through the preliminaries of love with a constantly changing series of new people. I can go deeper, uncover new levels of intimacy with him that help me know myself better. What I learn from marriage carries over into my relationships with others. It helps me reach out and form deeper friendships.

Of course, as a married woman, I am still attracted to other men, just as I imagine a monk continues to struggle with the temptations of the flesh. But though it is not always easy, my commitment to Angus keeps me free from destructive entanglement with others, and I find a different kind of freedom in the possibilities that intimacy affords.

Commitment to work is much the same. Whether it is one all-consuming career or, as in my case, a few selected activities, by choosing, by dedicating myself to the tasks at hand, I can focus my energies, go deeper, and use my talents in ways that are satisfying. If I can learn to sort out the voices of desire, ego, ambition, and power from the voice of true self-expression, I am free to become who I really am. Still, it is hard to resist the calls to more involvement, to say no to the demands for my time. A monastery helps control the voices and choices. In the world, we have to set our own limits and make our own walls.

Just how committed should we be? I often worry that my multiple careers, the variety of activities that I have built into my life, are keeping me from real depth, and that I should have adopted one lifework and stayed with it.

Commitment is rarely simple or easy to maintain. Thomas Merton's struggle with himself did not end when he entered the Trappist monastery. As the years passed, the world seemed to hold on tighter and would not let him go. He had expected, for example, that after he became a monk, his desire to be a writer would fade, and that he would redirect his energies to activities within the walls of the abbey. To the contrary, he wrote more and more, and his superiors encouraged his work. He struggled for years with his growing fame and its implications for a life that was supposed to be rooted in humility and dedicated to God.

Merton struggled also with the conflict between solitude and community. He desperately sought solitude and eventually convinced his superiors to let him build a small hermitage on the grounds of the monastery, where he could pray and write undisturbed. But he was much in demand, both in the abbey and outside its walls, and he was drawn inexorably into engagement and connection. He corresponded with Dorothy Day, with Pope John XXIII, and with dozens of other people. He began to speak out on issues like nonviolence and world peace. He became increasingly interested in Eastern religious thought and in strengthening the bonds between contemplatives the world over. In 1968, Merton embarked on a trip to Asia: to India, where he met with the Dalai Lama, to Sri Lanka, to Singapore, and finally to Thailand for a conference of contemplatives. After delivering a paper on the morning of 9 December, he returned to his room and died, electrocuted by a defective fan.

Reading about Merton's attraction to Eastern thought raised an old issue for me, that of freedom of belief. I was brought up in an atmosphere in which free thought—what was new, what was challenging—deserved to be met with an open mind. Orthodoxy or creed was anathema. This inherited bias toward "freedom," coupled with my interest in Eastern religion, stopped me initially from wanting to commit to Christianity. Would becoming a Christian limit my options?

But belief, I am discovering, is not unlike work or relationships. If I dabble, take a little from here and a little from there, I am endlessly fascinated, but unfulfilled. On the other hand, by making a personal commitment to Christianity, I can enter, heart and soul, into its depths. I can discover that the very act of commitment changes the quality of the experience and engages me at a new level. The addition of belief, the leap of faith, does not close out options but opens new doors. It does not mean that Christianity is right, and other paths are wrong. Like Thomas Merton, I may still gain new insight and wisdom from other traditions that can deepen my understanding of my own. They are all like spokes on a wheel, any one of which can provide a way to the center. Commitment is what gives us the heart for the journey and opens a path before us.

Though reading Thomas Merton never fails to make me long for the peace and spiritual depth that I imagine I would find in a monastery, I am unlikely to choose the monastic life. I love my husband and my family. I love my work in the world. But I need, like the residents of the abbey, to surround myself with walls. I build a fence around my garden and pull out basketfuls of weeds, in order to give space to my plants and protect them from invaders and predators of various kinds. In the same way, by limiting my options, by focusing on a chosen path, I silence the distractions and resist being shaped by compulsion, by power, by applause. I build walls, but they are the walls of freedom, those that will let me flower and become who I really am.

Epilogue
(with inspiration from T. S. Eliot)

"There is no end of it . . . / no end to the withering of withered flowers," writes T. S. Eliot in the third of his *Four Quartets*. Indeed, it seems like only yesterday that the first yellow daffodils around the lake near our house opened their glowing faces to the afternoon sun, and now they are withering. One by one, they are browning at the edges, turning tissue thin, and curling back into the bulbs from which they came. The crocuses and scylla are all gone now, and even the tulips are looking tired, beginning to relax their petals and showing signs of decline.

But this withering, this ending, is only the beginning. This dying back is just a necessary stage in the renewal process that will bring the next generation of flowers into bloom again a year from now. I am not depressed by the withering. There is too much summer ahead to have any regrets.

How different I feel from a year ago when I identified with the tiny seedlings in my new summer garden, when I longed for time, for roots and rest. Is it only the passing of a year, the completion of a cycle in the garden? I don't think so. I think it has something to do with the company I've kept for the last twelve months, the words of wisdom that I have absorbed.

I have had steady support from the mentors in my life, as well as those from history whom I shall never meet. My friend Nancy no longer seems to speak in a foreign language. She and I have begun to see eye to eye, to share books and insights, and our friendship is stronger than it ever was.

My friend the bishop has retired, and he now lives in another state. At first I was afraid of losing him, afraid that somehow my spiritual life depended on him, that he was not only a mentor but a medium. I have found to the contrary that I have grown in his absence. I have continued to study, to write, and to be drawn to the spiritual life however it presents itself. We keep in touch, and I hope we always will, but his leaving was an important step at a time when I needed, perhaps more than his guidance, encouragement to find my own way.

I have found other guides as well. I have traveled back as far as the fifth century and steeped myself in the thoughts and writings of mystics and sages over a span of more than fifteen hundred years. I've read the words of men and women who were saints, monks, and ordinary people of extraordinary insight. Each encounter has provoked thought, raised questions, and shed light in some way to help me see where I am going.

This exploration has led me to examine many aspects of my own spiritual life. I needed to balance my study of yoga and a leaning toward Eastern mysticism with a broad exposure to Christian spirituality, one that could help me take root in my own religious tradition. I needed to be convinced that Christianity—its teachings and its teachers—could offer something of tangible value to a North American woman in the 1990s.

My response to these spiritual giants has been varied. A few have become mentors or models for me. From others I have benefited more by my reaction against what they had to say.

From Egeria, a fifth-century pilgrim, I received courage and heart for the journey. The sheer physical impossibility of her own pilgrimage to the Holy Land has given me strength for my own quest. Her silence about the reasons for her trip has forced me to articulate my own and to pose the questions that can guide me along the way.

Augustine's *Confessions* helped me to recognize that I have undergone a major midlife shift in the way that I perceive the world. Augustine allowed me to see that I have moved away from logical, analytical patterns of thought to a way of thinking that is more intuitive and metaphorical, that emanates from the heart rather than exclusively from the head.

Saint Benedict taught me about balance and reinforced for me the importance of redistributing the weight I had given to the various parts of my life. I learned from his Rule for life in a monastery to seek a more equal allocation of time for physical, intellectual, and spiritual activities, and to acknowledge that each reinforces and supports the other. Like Thomas Merton, Benedict has helped me understand the push and pull (and the interdependence) of solitude and community, of contemplation and action.

Julian of Norwich helped me to reclaim a portion of my life that had once seemed to represent nothing more than pain and suffering. Her vision of the unity that arises from paradox allowed me to see that only by embracing both sides of the human equation can we find truth. Out of suffering came new happiness; out of loneliness, community; out of weakness, strength.

My instinctive tendencies toward the path of inwardness and negation have been reinforced by the writings of Meister Eckhart, and he has articulated my own resistance to traditional characterizations of God. Eckhart, as well as Saints Catherine, John, and Teresa, have helped me to see my ego-driven will as an obstacle on the path to spiritual progress and have shown me that letting go, giving up the need to control, is critical.

Catherine of Siena, John of the Cross, and Teresa of Ávila all proposed different models for spiritual progress. Catherine and Teresa emphasized the importance of being rooted in self-knowledge and humility, and they both created vivid metaphors for the journey: the growth of a tree, and an interior castle containing successive rooms with walls of glass. For John, the journey is one through a series of Dark Nights—a vision as somber as Teresa's is dazzling—and he has let me know that the way will not be easy.

Martin Luther and Dorothy Day have forced me to examine the notion of good works and my own motivations for service. I am working toward the day when I give of myself not because doing so will earn points or reflect on my own reputation, but because I am drawn by love and no longer perceive the distinctions between my neighbor and me. With Martin Luther's and Dorothy Day's help, I am beginning to understand right action and to be equipped to discern which kinds of service make sense for me.

The Quakers, like the mystics, have shown me that silence is a strong tradition within Christianity, and they, along with Meister Eckhart, have reinforced my own instinctive leanings toward contemplative prayer. My explorations of the Quakers' rejection of ritual have led me to re-examine and reaffirm my own appreciation of the role of liturgy and sacrament in religious life.

Thomas Merton has invited me to explore the part of me that yearns for the solitude and peace of a monastery, and he has helped me to see that if I can learn to surrender my own ego, my false self, in a committed life outside the cloister walls, I too can move toward spiritual freedom.

I have benefited not only from these historical writings but from my own writing as well. The biggest surprise of this spiritual awakening for me has been the growing urge to write. I seem to need to give expression to these interior changes of mine. I need an outlet, and my hands, the pen, and the keyboard are the tools of choice. Each one of these spiritual writers has come alive for me when I have taken a piece of my own life and held it up to the light of their thought and wisdom.

Writing is a way of taking their energy and mine, and together letting them create something new—a layer of meaning they did not have before. Writing, it turns out, is how I find out what I think. I trust that voice that seems to come from nowhere. T. S. Eliot says:

> We had the experience but missed the meaning,
> And approach to the meaning restores the experience
> In a different form. . . .

Reflection intensifies experience, gives it depth and resonance. It lifts the raw material of our lives briefly out of time and space, holds it in suspension, and exposes it to a kind of eternal light.

"In my end is my beginning," writes Eliot. Though I have come through a long and fruitful year, in many ways I have just begun. I have only scratched the surface of the Bible, and there is a long list of writers—both Christian and non-Christian . . . that I am eager to read. "Home is where one starts from," and clearly I am still under the influence of my earlier biases. I find myself apologizing in some circles for my spiritual bent and, in particular, my Christian orientation. I wince when the word *Christian* is used as a synonym for good, or when so-called Christians strike out in anger or intolerance against views or lifestyles that don't match their own. I am more comfortable with agnostics than with Christians who are rigid and self-righteous in their point of view.

Though I am beginning to understand the dynamics of the cross and feel its rhythms in the ups and downs of my life, I am still a long way from internalizing a Christocentric theology. I am comfortable with the liturgy, but I haven't let Christ become part of my own personal vocabulary.

I am still very much a woman of the world, one who lives to satisfy her own ego, to exercise power and exert her own will. I am a long way from surrender: from letting go, from receiving and doing God's will. Though I have embarked on the path to self-knowledge, humility is a distant goal. Despite all this, I know there is no turning back.

When I look back over the last few years—years of growth and mysterious change—I see that the outlines of my life are the same. My family is the same. My friends, for the most part, have not changed. I live in the same house, and I work for the same organizations and causes.

But from another perspective, everything has changed. The focus has shifted away from the world outside. The center of gravity has moved to the still point within. . . . "Except for the point, the still point, / There would be no dance, and there is only the dance," says Eliot. It is ironic, but as I have uncovered this new depth, this centerpoint, as I have learned to come to stillness and silence, a new, unexpected energy has emerged. The writing, the creative activity, was never there before. The new publishing venture, an effort to bring the creative work of others to the world at large, is there. And I notice new energy in my work at the Guthrie Theater and in my relationships with the people I meet in day-to-day life. As T. S. Eliot writes in "Little Gidding":

> We shall not cease from exploration
> And the end of all our exploring
> Will be to arrive where we started
> And know the place for the first time.

Acknowledgments

The scriptural quotes cited in this book are from the New Revised Standard Version of the Bible. Copyright © 1989 by the Division of Christian Education of the National Council of the Churches of Christ in the United States of America. All rights reserved.

Prologue
The excerpt on pages 15–16 is from *Journal of a Solitude,* by May Sarton (New York: W. W. Norton and Company, 1973), page 81. Copyright © 1973 by May Sarton.

The excerpt on page 17 is from *The Road Less Traveled: A New Psychology of Love, Traditional Values and Spiritual Growth,* by M. Scott Peck, MD (New York: Simon and Schuster, 1978), page 223. Copyright © 1978 by M. Scott Peck, MD.

June
The excerpts on pages 23, 23–24, and 24 are from *Egeria: Diary of a Pilgrimage,* number 38 of *Ancient Christian Writers: The Works of the Fathers in Translation,* translated and annotated by George E. Gingras (New York: Newman Press, 1970), pages 59; 82; and 83, 87, and 66; respectively. Copyright © 1970 by Rev. Johannes Quasten, Rev. Walter J. Burghardt, SJ, and Thomas Comerford Lawler. Used by permission of Paulist Press.

July
The excerpt on page 31 is from *The Portable Jung,* edited by Joseph Campbell (New York: Penguin Books, 1971), pages 16–17. Copyright © 1971 by Viking Penguin.

The excerpts on pages 33, 34, 34–35, 35, 38, and 39 are from *The Confessions of St. Augustine,* translated by Rex Warner (New York: Penguin Books, 1963), pages 116; 108–109; 116; 175, 182, 194; 17; and 150; respectively. Translation copyright © 1963 by Rex

Warner, renewed 1991 by F. C. Warner. Introduction copyright © 1963, renewed 1991 by Vernon J. Bourke. Used by permission of Dutton Signet, a division of Penguin Books U.S.A.

The excerpts on page 37 are from *What Is Anglicanism?* by Urban T. Holmes III (Harrisburg, PA: Morehouse Publishing, 1982), page 4. Copyright © 1982 by Jane Neighbors Holmes.

August

The excerpts on pages 43 (first excerpt) and 45 are from *Living with Contradiction: Reflections on the Rule of St. Benedict,* by Esther de Waal (San Francisco: Harper and Row, 1989), pages 6 and 102. Copyright © 1989 by Esther de Waal.

The excerpts on pages 43 (second excerpt), 44, and 49 are from *The Rule of St. Benedict,* translated by Anthony C. Meisel and M. L. del Mastro (New York: Doubleday Image, 1975), pages 86; 86, 87, 66, 47; and 53; respectively. Copyright © 1975 by Anthony C. Meisel and M. L. del Mastro. Used by permission of Doubleday, a division of Bantam Doubleday Dell Publishing Group.

September

The excerpts on pages 52, 53, 53–54, 54, 55, 56, and 58 are from *Julian of Norwich: Showings,* translated by Edmund Colledge and James Walsh (New York: Paulist Press, 1978), pages 127; 129, 133, 165, 144, 132–133; 299; 225; 228, 179; 205; and 225; respectively. Copyright © 1978 by the Missionary Society of St. Paul the Apostle in the State of New York. Used by permission of the publisher.

October

The excerpt on page 59 is from *Meister Eckhart: The Essential Sermons, Commentaries, Treatises and Defense,* translated and edited by Edmund Colledge, OSA, and Bernard McGinn, preface by Huston Smith (New York: Paulist Press, 1981), page xiii. Copyright © 1981 by the Missionary Society of St. Paul the Apostle in the State of New York.

The excerpts on pages 60 and 61 (second excerpt) are from *Meister Eckhart: A Modern Translation,* by Raymond Bernard Blakney (New York: Harper and Row, 1941), pages xxiii and 85. Copyright © 1941 by Harper and Row, Publishers.

The first excerpt on page 61 is from *Meister Eckhart: The Mystic as Theologian,* by Robert K. C. Forman (Rockport, MA:

Element, 1991), page 70. Copyright © 1991 by Robert K. C. Forman.

The excerpts on pages 61 (third, fourth, fifth, and sixth excerpts), 62, and 63 are from *Breakthrough: Meister Eckhart's Creation Spirituality in New Translation,* introduction and commentaries by Matthew Fox (New York: Doubleday Image Books, 1980), pages 178, 178, 181, 180; 169, 179, 218; 177 and 209; respectively. Copyright © 1980 by Matthew Fox. Used by permission of Doubleday, a division of Bantam Doubleday Dell Publishing Group.

November

The excerpts on pages 68, 70 (third excerpt), 71, 72, and 73 are from *Catherine of Siena: The Dialogue,* translated by Suzanne Noffke, OP, preface by Giuliana Cavallini (New York: Paulist Press, 1980), pages 40; 29; 85; 41–42, 160; 162 and 165; respectively. Copyright © 1980 by the Missionary Society of St. Paul the Apostle in the State of New York. Used by permission of the publisher.

The first, second, and fourth excerpts on page 70 are quoted from *Enduring Grace: Living Portraits of Seven Women Mystics,* by Carol Lee Flinders (San Francisco: HarperSanFrancisco, 1993), pages 110, 111, and 111, respectively. Copyright © 1993 by Carol Flinders. Used with permission of HarperCollins Publishers.

December

The excerpts on pages 77, 79, and 80 (second and third excerpts) are from *John of the Cross: Selected Writings,* edited by Kieran Kavanaugh, OCD, preface by Ernest E. Larkin, O CARM (New York: Paulist Press, 1987), pages 163; 166, 179, 181; and 185; respectively. Copyright © 1987 by the Washington Province of Discalced Carmelite Friars. Used by permission of the publisher.

The first excerpt on page 80 is from *Dark Night of the Soul by St. John of the Cross,* translated and edited by E. Allison Peers (New York: Doubleday Image Books, 1990), page 132.

January

The excerpts on pages 82, 84 (first excerpt), 86, 87, 88, 89 (first, second, and fourth excerpts), and 90 are from *Teresa of Ávila: The Interior Castle,* translated by Kieran Kavanaugh, OCD, and Otilio Rodriguez, OCD, preface by Raimundo Panikkar (New York: Paulist Press, 1979), pages 35; 2; 39; 45, 46; 49, 55, 57; 68, 52, 70; 178 and 190; respectively. Copyright © 1979 by the Washington

Province of Discalced Carmelite Friars. Used by permission of the publisher.

The excerpts on pages 83 and 84 (second excerpt) are from *Enduring Grace,* by Carol Lee Flinders, pages 171 and 169. Used with permission.

The third excerpt on page 89 is from *Tao Te Ching,* translated by Stephen Mitchell (New York: HarperPerennial, 1991), page 16. Translation copyright © 1988 by Stephen Mitchell.

February

The excerpts on pages 92 and 99 are from *Martin Luther: Three Treatises,* second revised edition, translated by Charles Jacobs (Philadelphia: Fortress Press, 1970), pages 296, 282, 297, 305; and 295; respectively. Second revised edition copyright © 1970 by Fortress Press. Reprinted from *The American Edition of Luther's Works,* copyright © 1943 by Muhlenberg Press. Used by permission of Augsburg Fortress.

The excerpts on page 93 are from *A World Lit Only by Fire: The Medieval Mind and the Renaissance, Portrait of an Age,* by William Manchester (Boston: Little, Brown and Company, 1992), pages 137–138 and 158. Copyright © 1992, 1993 by William Manchester.

The excerpt on page 94 is from *Christian Spirituality: High Middle Ages and Reformation,* edited by Jill Raitt in collaboration with Bernard McGinn and John Meyendorff (New York: Crossroad, 1988), page 273. Copyright © 1987 by the Crossroad Publishing Company.

March

The excerpts on pages 102, 103, 105, 106, 107, and 108 are from *Quaker Spirituality: Selected Writings,* edited and introduced by Douglas V. Steere, preface by Elizabeth Gray Vining (New York: Paulist Press, 1984), pages 149, 132; 73; 27, 156; 250, 99; 69, 257, 85; and 42; respectively. Copyright © 1984 by Douglas V. Steere. Used by permission of the publisher.

April

The excerpts on pages 113, 114, 117, and 118 are from *The Long Loneliness: The Autobiography of Dorothy Day* (San Francisco: HarperSanFrancisco, 1952), pages 42, 43; 95, 140, 171; 214; and 204; respectively. Copyright © 1952 by Harper and Row, Publishers. Copyright © renewed 1980 by Tamar Teresa Hennessy. Introduc-